STEP

ON *Faith:*

CAN GOD CONSIDER YOU?

by

Katrina Marie

BLACKSEEDS
Publishing

Printed in the United States of America

ISBN-13: 978-1-7366613-7-6

Disclaimer: Some names have been changed to protect the privacy of those involved. There are, however, real names of amazing individuals have gave permission to be used in my story. A special thanks to the Brown family, Jamie Hopkins, Grace Williams, Chad and Brooke Seabright, Jackie Scott, and Stacey and Ely Roberts.

KATRINA MARIE

BLACKSEEDS
Publishing

The Brown Family

CashApp: $Encourager79

Table of Contents

Dedication

~

I dedicate this book to my mom; Anita Hunter, Grandmother, Minnie O'Neal, and Great Grandmother; Virginia Edwards. Though you all are no longer with me, your legacy will continue through me.

I pray that The Most High will give me the grace to keep our family legacy alive. You all were loving and caring and showed me what faith in God could do. You taught me how to stay strong and stay the course no matter what I was facing.

Trust God is what you instilled in me, and because I listened, I was able to make it through the wilderness without giving up. My heart's desire has always been to love, care for, encourage, and uplift others. You instilled

By Katrina Marie

that in me, and I am grateful. I hope I have made you proud.

I also dedicate this book to my family. I love you all deeply and pray for you constantly. It is my heart's desire to see you healed, delivered, and free. Your identity is found in The Most High. When you seek after Him with your whole heart, you will find yourself. May your latter days be greater than your beginning.

†††

Last but certainly not least, I want to dedicate this book to my husband, Marvin Brown, and my children, Delvin, K'Shiya, and KaMarviun. I made it through this faith journey because I had my family by my side. We kept each other encouraged and always prayed together.

When I was weak and tired and felt like giving up, you all reminded me that God got us, and the strength and power I needed to keep going was inside of me. I love you all dearly!

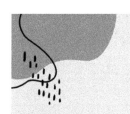

Katrina Marie
@katrinamarie

Now faith is the substance of things hoped for, the evidence of things not seen.

#SteppingOutOnFaith
#CanGodConsiderYou

Hebrews 11:1
(King James Version)

Prelude

I have this feeling deep down inside me that just won't go away. I have had this feeling for a long time, but it has gotten stronger over the years.

The more I try to ignore it, the stronger it gets. It feels like something trying to burst out of me. It is even hard to try and explain this feeling.

All I know is that it will not leave me alone. It causes me to cry sometimes and get frustrated and confused all at the same time.

I do not understand what is wrong with me. I have anxiety attacks, and my mind is having conversations I have not been invited to. I think I am losing my mind. I cannot tell anyone about this because they may laugh, not take me seriously, or my family may think I need to be admitted to a mental institution.

So, I call on my Father in Heaven because I need answers, help, and peace of mind. I feel so drawn to Him. God has always been a part of my life, even when I did not understand everything about Him. All I know is that I accepted Him as my Lord and Savior when I was younger.

There was this connection we had once I accepted Him into my life. Sometimes the connection was strong, sometimes it was weak, and sometimes it felt like there was no connection at all. No Power at All! It was in those times I believed God was working even when I could not see it or feel it because He is always working.

Even though I was struggling with something in me, I always felt drawn to help others and share God's love with them. Anytime someone was going through life struggles, I felt led to pray for them and help them.

If they were down, I would encourage them and uplift their

spirit. When they felt like giving up on life, I was there to comfort them and give them a sense of hope. No one asked me to do it. I just felt led by the Spirit to do it. I get so much joy from sharing God's Word and love with others.

It brings me great joy just to see the smile on others face when they realize someone cares enough about them to speak life to them.

But at the same time... so many questions were running through my mind.

What is this feeling? Why am I being pulled in that direction?

God cannot be calling me to the ministry!

- ▷ I was damaged from being molested as a child!

- ▷ I do not know who my father is!

- ▷ I am confused about who I am!

- ▷ I ran away from home!

- ▷ I had a baby at 17!

My mind is not stable, and I had suicidal thoughts! I spent most of my life hiding in the darkness, weak and afraid.

What would people think?!!!!!

God answered, "Yes... You!"

✝✝✝

As I pondered, God reminded me that He was using me to show others how He brought me out of all that darkness and into His marvelous light. The pain I endured in my life was to help those who needed to know that God can mold and make them into something extraordinary.

God can take the worst of you and your life and create something beautiful. God knew that I would have a marvelous testimony when He was done. See, that feeling I was having, God placed in me. It was His Spirit.

That is why the feeling would not go away. It was my gift and purpose being stirred up in me. It wants burst out of me.

I just did not know how to let it.

There is a calling on my life by God. He is calling me to fulfill the purpose He created me for.

See, I know there is an anointing over my life, which has been for a long time. How did I get started? God wanted me to surrender completely to Him and His will for my life.

I needed to trust the path He had already predestined me to take. I knew it was time to step out on faith and trust God. Even though I did not know what I was stepping into, I had to trust God's process for me.

Remember, He was the One who put this gift in me. He is my Creator, so He knows all about me.

It makes sense that God was using the hurt and pain I experienced to help save others and draw them closer to Him.

> **He wanted you to know you can be healed, restored, made whole, set free, and live again.**

See, instead of people seeing me, they would see GOD working in and through me.

They will see how God was changing me and that I am not the same Katrina.

A new me is springing forth.

I'm a servant of the Most High.

This is my ministry.

✝✝✝

I am a living Testimony!

Just as much as God loved me, I desperately wanted and needed Him. I was tired of existing and having no sense of direction.

The Lord is my Shepard; I just need to let Him lead.

All I know is I wanted to live. I knew there was much more to my life than where I was.

My life here on earth was no mistake. God created me for a purpose, and I will fulfill it.

I had to say, "Not my will, Lord, but let Your Will be done in my life."

✝✝✝

It was time to stop running FROM God and run TO God.

I am not sure where this journey will take me, but I know I can put all of my faith and trust in God. He will lead and guide me in the right direction.

No matter where or what happens in my life, God promised He would always be with me. That was the comfort I needed if fear tried to creep in (and it did).

There may be some trials, tribulations, storms, setbacks, tears, frustration, obstacles, loneliness, pain, and times that I might want to give up, but I will trust the plan and process God has for me because I know He is positioning me for Greatness.

So, as I am taking this leap of faith, I wanted to share my testimony of the miracles, blessings, favor, people, growth, and opportunities God has given my family because we SURRENDERED to Him and STEPPED OUT on faith.

Enjoy our journey! See, if you trace God's hand moving in our life, my prayer is that my testimony will be life-changing for YOU.

STEPPING OUT

ON *Faith:*

CAN GOD CONSIDER YOU?

by

Katrina Marie

BLACKSEEDS
Publishing

Katrina Marie
@katrinamarie

And be not conformed to this world: but be ye transformed by the renewing of your mind, that ye may prove what is that good, and acceptable, and perfect, will of God.

#SteppingOutOnFaith
#CanGodConsiderYou

Romans 12:2
(King James Version)

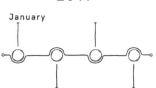

Chapter 1

How It All Began

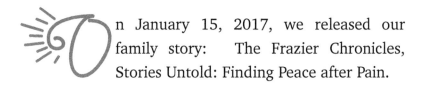

n January 15, 2017, we released our family story: The Frazier Chronicles, Stories Untold: Finding Peace after Pain.

Becoming a co-author of this book was a significant milestone in my life because it allowed me to share with the world about my being molested at a young age and being taken from my mom. It gave readers a summary of how I made it.

So many breakthroughs and healing were made after the release of that book. My voice was heard, and I was no longer shamed to talk about what happened to me.

Now, I know you are thinking I should be good now because I got it all out, but I was not. See, I knew in my heart that was just the beginning of my journey.

†††

See, for all of my life, I settled.

I was existing and passing the time.

My outside appearance seemed like everything was okay, but deep down inside, I was drowning from the tears inside.

I had all the right things to say to help encourage *others,* but never had anything positive to say to *myself.* I was constantly pouring out to *others,* but had no one pouring back into *me.*

I knew I was different, and came to terms with it.

I did not think, talk, or even dress like everyone else. That was one of the main reasons kids would tease me when I was younger. They called my hair 'nappy', called me ugly, and said I dressed like my grandma.

Those words did hurt, but I could not be mad at them. I still wanted to show myself friendly to them. Why didn't I just give them a piece of my mind? Because it was not in my character. I showed them mercy even before I knew what it was. My Father created me this way. It is one of my gifts.

I knew God had to have something great in store for me. This could not be 'it' for my life!

I felt like I was on a merry-go-round… going in circles.

When is MY time? When will I get ahead?

God said, "Surrender yourself completely to Me. Then and only then can you walk in your full potential."

✝✝✝

God makes no mistakes. He made me different for a reason. I am His Masterpiece! He took His time to mold and shape me into what He would have me to be.

He created me to be strong, bold, confident, resilient, unstoppable, unlovable, courageous, and a woman of faith.

Even when I could not see Him, feel Him, or things in my life was 'quiet', He was underground moving on my behalf!

God allowed me to go through the pain because He knew I could handle it. He knew my testimony would help save lives all around the world, and allow people to see Him in a way they have never seen.

I used to struggle daily about my purpose. I had a great job, making decent money. My husband loved me, and my kids adored me. Our bills were always paid, and we even had money saved. So, I should be okay, right?

For a person who just wanted to barely make it, or only have enough to be comfortable... yes, but I wanted more. I needed more. I didn't know what the "more" was at that point.

Even though I had a good job, I still had an empty feeling. My job was not my destiny.

Do I quit my job? I had a family to care for, so I could not just *quit* my job. I needed to make a sound decision and weigh the costs. This empty feeling inside was nagging me.

See, my good job came with a sacrifice. I rarely was able to spend time with my family. My kids spent most of their time with my in-laws, or home alone when they were old enough.

Just to top it all off, I had not been to church on Sunday in about maybe five years. I needed to get back to church so I could get a closer relationship with God. I needed God in my life, and there was no way possible that I was going to make it without Him.

So, my husband and I started talking about relocating and starting over. He was also beginning to feel that it was much more to his life than working to pay the bills.

My husband was working over 96 hours a week straight to bring money into the house. That was great and all, but it required him to be gone all the time. He was an Emergency Medical Technician (EMT) and was a darn good one! He was so gifted at it. But him being gone all the time made me feel single, even though I was married.

My bed used to feel lonely at night without him, and the kids did not get to see him much either. It was circumstances like those that caused us to reconsider our lives because it seemed our family was drifting apart.

Our lives were not matching what God had said.

✝✝✝

So, too fast forward to January 2017, my husband, kids, and I visited my brother and sister-in-law in Nashville, Tennessee. We discussed with them our relocation plans, and they showed us around the town. We first went to

Mount Juliet, Tennessee. The area was nice and reminded us of 'home'. It felt like this was where we should be.

Now, take it that this was our plan, but we did not know how it would happen. We prayed together, touched and agreed, and returned to our lives.

†††

One night we attended church service with our previous Pastor in Memphis, Tennessee. That night service was different than any other we've attended. A prophet whom we'd never met before prophesied to us.

He looked at me and said that God gave him a hurricane. He asked my name, I told him. Then he looked over at my husband and stated matter of factly, "You used to have anger issues." My husband nodded yes.

The prophet then told us that a *shift* was going to take place in our lives in the next six months: we would receive a house, we would be able to breathe, and I would be a great help to the Kingdom of God.

We received the prophesy from the man of God, and went back to our everyday lives.

-The prophecy was given to us in January 2017-

†††

Well, let me tell you, some changes were beginning to happen. My husband's company lost its contract with the county, so the workers had to find elsewhere to work.

My husband just ended up transferring to another county his company was still in, not knowing they would lose their contract as well. After working in Batesville, Mississippi for two weeks, he was told that the company was shutting down in 30 days.

What were we going to do?

Well, my husband was then transferred to Nashville, Tennessee, and may I add that he was also given a $5 raise.

Can you say, "Increase!"

As we looked back and remembered, it was 6 months from the day we were prophesied about a shift taking place. God was opening a door to relocate and have a fresh start. Little did we know about the journey we were getting ready to take.

†††

We still had some time before relocating, so I began looking for jobs in Tennessee. I was working at the casino. Every day I woke up deciding whether I was going to work or not. I knew I was no longer happy.

Every time my season ended at the place where I was working(serving), I got this feeling that it was time to move on.

My husband had already finished his last day at work and was waiting to go to his orientation in Nashville. The thought of him being home alone and that made the decision easy. You got it, I quit!

Believe it or not, on my last day of work at the casino, I felt free. I could have worked until my husband started his job, but I had to step out on faith. I did not know what I was stepping out in to, but I knew I trusted God and wanted to experience all He had for me.

†††

My husband and I started looking for places to stay in Tennessee. We even made a couple of trips to look at houses. We found this lovely townhome and decided it was the one.

My husband applied for the townhouse, but we were $200 short on the income requirement. So, to show you how God works, I met some incredible ladies while at my previous employment at the casino.

We became close. They were just like family and reminded me of my grandma. For them to be in their 70s, they got around well. Talking about God will bring people into your life that you did not know were created for you... how ironic they both were from the area we were relocating to!

I called one of my good friends and explained to her about the issues we were having trying to find a place to stay. She gave me a couple of leads to call, and sent me a few houses. To no avail.

I know you are thinking, maybe this is a sign to not move.

I did not believe that. I believed God opened the door for my husband to transfer to Nashville because that was our ticket to get to where He was taking us.

The enemy was just trying to scare us into staying so we would never receive God's promise.

Time was winding down, and we still did not have a place to stay.

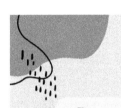

Katrina Marie
@katrinamarie

Now the Lord had said unto Abram, Get thee out of thy country, and from thy kindred, and from thy father's house, unto a land that I will shew thee.

#SteppingOutOnFaith
#CanGodConsiderYou

Genesis 12:1
(King James Version)

Chapter 2

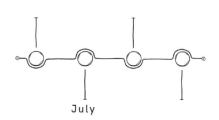

July

The New Journey Begins

t was July 27, 2017. That's Right! It was moving day, and we had not found a house yet.

It did not matter because we trusted God would guide us where we needed to be. So, we packed up the U-haul and headed to Mount Juliet, Tennessee, without a place to stay.

Crazy Right?

No!

When you have faith in God, anything is possible. We even had family members tell us to leave our kids behind and send for them once we were settled.

We were a family, and family sticks together. We are stronger together, and, besides, my kids would not allow me to leave them behind anyway.

✝✝✝

While we were driving to Mount Juliet, I made phone calls to search for an apartment. Only one answered, and they had exactly what we needed, a 3-bedroom apartment; but the office closed at 6:00 p.m. Needless to say, we were pushing it to get there.

I prayed, "Lord, please let us get there on time."

Heart pounding the entire time, praying and pushing the pedal to the medal, we pulled into the parking lot at 5:30 p.m.

We were cutting it close! We went in and filled out the application. We were approved immediately! We paid our deposit and toured the apartment. We told the agent we would take it. So, the agent asked, "When do you want to move in?" We knew we had nowhere else to go, and we had a U-haul full of furniture.

My husband and I said together, "Today!"

The agent replied, "I usually do not do this, but okay."

Hallelujah! Praise God! God just made a way out of no way! God showed us favor with the agent.

We moved in, and our new journey in a new place had begun.

We registered the kids for school, and they were transitioning very well.

†††

So, I know you are probably thinking, "They relocated, found a place to stay, husband is working, hmm, looks like everything is going great!" Right? Well, not yet!

You see, I still had not found a job yet. I spent the first month going to the library every morning, searching online job databases, and filling out job applications. I filled out so many applications that I lost count.

Crickets. Nothing. Silence.

I know I was qualified for most of the jobs I applied to. One company told me I was 'under-qualified'. It only paid $8 an hour, and I was wondering exactly what qualification do you need to just answer a phone?

I had a few offers from fast food restaurants, but I wanted to do something different. I felt 20 years in the food industry was enough. There was more to me than just food. I wanted to be in an office setting.

I applied for office jobs, including some agency temporary services. Nothing!

The more I went to the library to fill out and submit job applications, the more stressed I became, and I could feel my anxiety starting up again.

See, before we moved, I prayed to God that I wanted doors to open for me that would lead me to my destiny. I did not just want a job, but I wanted what He had for me.

I also put in a special request to have the weekend off. I wanted to spend more time with my family, and my previous jobs wouldn't allow me to be home some nights.

✝✝✝

Now, where was I? Oh, yeah, putting in job applications. So, I decided to give myself a break from putting in applications.

Who knew that I would have so much peace once I did that?! Whew, a weight was lifted from that decision to take a break from the vicious job hunt!

I realized that just because I wasn't clocking in on someone else's clock, didn't mean I didn't have work to do! I had a family, thus all of my attention went into taking care of my family. Serving them.

I got to be a wife and a mother.

It was a great feeling. Something I always wanted to do. I also used the time to get closer to God by studying the Bible, praying, and fasting.

The more I spent time with my Father, the more I could feel His presence.

Wait! Something was messing with me. What was it? It was my purpose that kept creeping up.

It was that inner feeling bubbling inside. God was calling me into ministry. A sense of fear came all over me.

I did not respond to my Father, and I could not sleep for a full week. I cried, pleaded, and prayed.

Then I fell on my knees with my hands lifted and head bowed with tears falling and mucus coming out my nose, and I said, "Alright, Father, I completely surrender my life to You. My heart, soul, and mind say YES to Your Will."

You can imagine the weight lifted when I surrendered all to God; after that, I could sleep again.

Father knows how to get our attention.

REMINDER

Our Father knows how to get our attention.
All it takes is your YES!

@katrinamarie   #TheEncourager

Using the camera on my phone, I started recording videos and uploading them to our private Facebook group. I just wanted to share some encouraging words God had placed in my heart.

I enjoyed doing that (recording the videos). It brought me such great joy. So instead of focusing so much on what my purpose was, I focused on what gave me the most joy and fulfillment.

It was serving others, encouraging, speaking life, helping others, and offering hope.

It was helping others change their mindsets from negative to positive and declaring and sharing God's Word.

That brought me more joy than you know.

✝✝✝

See, everyone has a ministry. It does not have to be behind a pulpit. I would rather minister outside of the church because those would be the ones who had either been hurt by the church or sworn off church altogether.

Truth be told, we are the church, and the place everyone attends on Sunday is the church building.

Some people may disagree with this, but it is okay. This is my testimony.

✝✝✝

I am starting to learn that the purpose behind my pain was so that I could help those who have gone through what I did. In those times that I am healing others, I am healing myself all at the same time.

I realized it was okay to dream big because God's Word says we have not because we ask not:

"Ye lust, and have not: ye kill, and desire to have, and cannot obtain: ye fight and war, yet ye have not, because ye ask not." (James 4:2 King James Version)

I had to take the limits off God and remove Him from the box I put Him in.

God is El Shaddai, a God of more than enough, which means He has unlimited resources. I believe God was doing big things in my life and my family's lives.

I am tired of only having just enough and living paycheck to paycheck. I decree and declare that my family will be wealthy, have abundance, prosper in every area of our lives, and walk in favor of God.

We are the reason we do not have in life because we have not realized that our words have power. What we speak is what we get. We must learn to shift our mindsets from negative to positive in order to change our lives.

When I started spending more time with God, and in His Word, it opened a different way of life for me. I was learning who I indeed was in Him. If God's Word said it, then I believed it.

My relationship with God increased, and I started seeing Him in ways I never had before. My faith was growing stronger, and I loved Him like I never had before.

REMINDER

In those times that I am healing others, I am healing myself all at the same time.

@katrinamarie   #TheEncourager

Who knew that our faith in God was getting ready to be tested?

†††

My husband's job transfer landed us in Tennessee, but we did not know God had *other* plans.

See, my husband thought he would be working five days a week as he was told, but after the transfer his schedule was bumped down to only 3 days a week— which meant less money than we originally budgeted for! My husband was not making enough to cover our $1600 monthly rent, and rent was due.

I wasn't working, and the only income we had was that of my husband. I could have started looking for a job, but that was not what my Father told me to do. *How was August rent going to get paid, plus all of the other bills?*

†††

We knew God did not open the door for us just to shut it in our face. So, we prayed to our Father to help us.

I started decreeing Philippians 4:19, And my God shall supply all our needs.

"But my God shall supply all your need according to His riches in glory by Christ Jesus." (Philippians 4:19)

God's Word said it, so I believed it. We continued our life like we knew God had it all handled.

Then we enjoyed the day until we received a late night reminder in our email inbox.

What do we do? We cannot get evicted already; we just got here. We cannot be homeless; we have kids to care for.

My husband noticed the look on my face and said just as calmly, "God got us, don't worry."

His voice calmed me enough to say, "Okay!"

Let me tell you that God did some supernatural miracle for us. The rent was paid! Hallelujah! We did not try to see who or how it got paid because we knew it was nobody but God. He gets ALL of the Glory!

†††

When we visited my brother and sister-in-law in January, we attended their church in Nashville.

The moment we stepped into the church, I knew I wanted to join, but we had not moved there yet.

22

Well, my family ended up joining the church in Nashville. We loved it there. I sang in the choir, my husband was part of the grief share ministry, and my kids were junior ushers.

Let me tell you the greatest joy there came when my children decided to give their life to Christ, and they were baptized on September 03, 2017. We were so excited!

We loved our church because even though we had not been there long, they made us feel welcomed and like part of the family.

Our Pastor could break down the Word like I had never seen. It was like God was using him to speak to me directly.

✝✝✝

I was able to attend a spiritual warfare class. I learned things that I never knew... for instance, *to know that Satan had been after me since my birth because even he knew the gifts my Father gave me.* His [Satan] job is to stop us from realizing who we are in Christ.

If you do not know your identity, then it is easy for Satan to trick you. Sometimes he will even disguise things to look like God so that when things blow up, you would be mad at God and not him, and thus lose your belief and faith in the One who created you.

That is why we need to study the enemy to be aware of the plots, tricks, and schemes he uses to get us off track and unfocused.

The only way to fight against the enemy is to be steps ahead of him.

✝✝✝

One of the other things we loved about our church was its outreach ministry. We were able to go out and volunteer in the community. We enjoyed the opportunity to fellowship with others outside the church.

You could sign up to volunteer at schools, nursing homes, etc. It brought my family great joy to be able to serve others. That church strongly believed in serving the community. We loved our church.

To be honest, attending church, singing in the choir, and helping others helped keep my faith up on this journey.

✝✝✝

My husband and I always loved looking at houses. We loved to go inside them and imagine living there. It also took our minds from what we were going through.

There was this one particular house that we toured, and we immediately fell in love with it. It was beautiful. My husband immediately said, "Baby, this is the house we were looking at online in Mississippi. This is our dream home."

As we toured the rest of the house, we immediately claimed that one day we would own a house like this.

REMINDER

It was in servitude where my faith was strengthened and renewed. As I served others.

@katrinamarie   #TheEncourager

My husband and I previously tried to buy a home in Mississippi. We did everything we could do and everything we were told to do even by realtors and bankers: We repaired our credit, paid off old debt little by little, built a nice savings account, and prayed to God for this home... yet we kept getting denied.

No matter how many times we got turned down, we just kept on applying. Then it all came together.

God was blocking those loans because He knew the plans He had for us was not in Mississippi. He knew He had other plans for our lives; we just needed to trust the process.

My husband, kids, and I prayed that God would bless us to be homeowners of a house like this one. We did not look at the price and say we could not buy it. We looked at the house and said, "Nothing is too hard for God!"

I know you are saying, "Why are you guys looking to buy a house when you couldn't even afford your rent?"

Well, because we knew we did not want to be in an apartment forever, our mindsets had changed from how we used to think. Romans 4:17 says, "call those things that are not as though they were."

"As it is written: "I have made you a father of many nations." He is our father in the sight of God, in whom he believed—the God who gives life to the dead and calls into being things that were not." (Romans 4:17 New International Version)

In the natural, the house was not mine, but, in the spirit, it was mine, and we had already moved in.

Plus, I could dream if I wanted to! We had faith in God's Word and that He would make His Word good. To show how much faith we had, we went furniture shopping for our future home!!

✝✝✝

I know you guys are thinking we must be off our rocker. No, we just have some crazy faith!

Faith is believing even when there is no evidence or proof of what you are believing for. If you can see it, then it is not faith.

We tried it our way so many times, and it did not work. We had to trust our Father because we knew He would never fail us. Not only did we believe in God for a house, but we believed in financial freedom.

Why not us? We always believe in something small but serve a loving, faithful, powerful God.

See, man can help you, but it is only so much they can do. God can do exceedingly, abundantly above and beyond all that we could ask or think according to the power that works in us.

"Now unto him that is able to do exceeding abundantly above all that we ask or think, according to the power that worketh in us." (Ephesians 3:20)

So, either we will believe the Word or not.

†††

I knew that if I was going to be everything my Father wanted me to be, I had to change my mindset and what I was speaking.

My mindset was one of the first places the enemy tried attacking, which would, in return, change what I was speaking. Our words have so much power, and the Bible tells us so.

"Death and life are in the power of the tongue: and they that love it shall eat the fruit thereof." (Proverbs 18:21)

So that means you can either speak blessings or curses in your life. We, The Brown Family, chose to speak life and be positive even when our situation seemed otherwise.

This step out on faith journey was not peaches and cream! Just because we believed in God and had faith did not stop us from going through trials and tribulations. It just gave us something to look forward to… Victory!

†††

September rent was due, and we still had the same budget. I was still unemployed but decided to start submitting job applications again. God did not tell me to, but I felt I needed to help my family financially.

Even though it seemed like we were in lack, we were giving our tithes to the church because that was how we were raised, and plus, I looked at us as *kingdom investors* instead.

> *"We were seed sowers, and we believed our seeds would eventually produce a bountiful harvest."*
> *-@KatrinaMarie*

Well, if you want to know if our rent was taken care of again, but of course! That is what we thought because we had not heard anything else.

God is faithful, and His Word will never return void. We could have been worrying, but worrying never positively affected us. It just keeps our faith wavering, sad, crying, and depressed.

I am not saying having faith was easy, but even with tears running down my face, I trusted God and asked for strength. The storm we were in had us tossing from side to side, front and back, up and down, and all around.

Bill collectors were knocking at the door and calling us. We had no money, and our bank accounts were depleted. All we had was each other and our faith in God and His Word to stand upon.

✝✝✝

A few times, we thought about reaching out to family, but we did not want to hear them say, "You should have never moved in the first place." Plus, the family could not do what we needed because many of them were going through hardships themselves.

The help would have been temporary, and God's help is eternal.

Sometimes you must move in silence until God gives you instructions on what to do. You are probably wondering why we did not pray and ask God to bring us out of the storm? Well, we thought about it, but we knew we would have a marvelous testimony when the storm was over.

We just once again asked God for strength to get through. There were also times we told God we needed some peace because the storm was raging havoc on us. It was in those moments that God stood amidst the storm with us and covered us with His protection.

†††

It's now October... I am still unemployed. No interviews. No callbacks. Nothing.

I could have just applied for any old job, which meant I would settle again. I was tired of doing that. I wanted whatever God's Will was for my life.

My heart, mind, and soul were still saying 'yes' to God. All of the pieces had not yet come together, but I knew as I began operating in my gift, little by little, God would increase me.

You must immediately start declaring God's Word when things in your life do not look like you will make it. It is our foundation. He is our Rock!

Even when bills came in, instead of dreading them, I looked at the bill and said, "You are paid in full." Even though in the natural, it was not paid—this was my way to stay positive so the enemy could not come into my mindset.

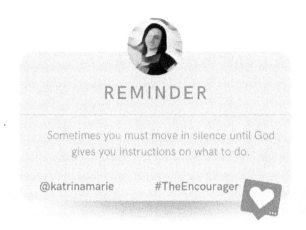

REMINDER

Sometimes you must move in silence until God gives you instructions on what to do.

@katrinamarie   #TheEncourager

What are you speaking over your life? Are you speaking Word of faith, or are you speaking words of defeat?

Remember, you have the power to change your life when you are seeking direction from God.

See, when the Most High created the world, He did it by *speaking*. We are made in His image and likeness, so we have some of His characteristics and power to speak.

"He replied, "Because you have so little faith. Truly I tell you, if you have faith as small as a mustard seed, you

can say to this mountain, 'Move from here to there,' and it will move. Nothing will be impossible for you." (Matthew 17:20 New International Version)

Everything you need in life is found in the Word. The answer is in the Word. You must purpose in your heart that you are tired of existing and want to LIVE!

To change my mindset, I not only read the Word and my bible plans, but I started reading other encouraging books that would help transform my mind so that I could be the best me possible.

- ▷ I wrote down affirmations that I spoke out loud daily.

- ▷ I wrote down declarations that I spoke over our lives and spent much time praying, meditating, and fasting.

We had to go through all this training to make it through this storm. Without God and training, we would have lost our minds, given up, and moved back to Mississippi, where we were *comfortable*.

Something else I did was write down my vision on paper.

Writing it down allowed me to continue to meditate on it. I probably would have forgotten about it if I had kept it in my mind.

Our lives get so busy that we tend to throw our dreams aside. Then before we know it, we stop dreaming. We end up just surviving, and I want to thrive. What about you?

I want to do things I never thought I could do. Habakkuk 2:2 says, "And the Lord answered me, and said, Write the vision, and make it plain upon tables, that he may run that readeth it."

But what really got me excited was verse 3. "For the vision is yet for an appointed time, but at the end it shall speak, and not lie: though it tarry, wait for it; because it will surely come, it will not tarry."

Oh my! This means **all my dreams will come true in due season**. Well, the ones that line up with my Father's Will, of course.

I just need to keep the faith.

You see, it's easy to ask your Father for

$50, but when you ask God for something *big*, some things you will go through that will require your faith to stand firm.

I told you this was **my step out on faith** season, and God worked in our lives. *Without Him, none of what I am sharing with you would be possible.*

✝✝✝

Everything seemed to be going alright. Well, we got an email that told us we needed to pay $3,657.05 by October 11, 2017, or we would be evicted.

At that moment, I knew we did not have the money, so I just looked at the email with tears running down my face and said, "Father nothing is too hard for you."

All I could do was repeat His Word back to Him.

"Is any thing too hard for the Lord? At the time appointed I will return unto thee, according to the time of life, and Sarah shall have a son." (Genesis 18:14)

THE ANSWER IS <u>NO</u>!

I believed if God brought us this far, He would continue to keep us. We are in the hands of God, and that is the best place to be!

†††

My Heavenly Father would never abandon His children. I really did not understand all that was going on, but if my family were together, I knew we would get through this season.

Our natural circumstances said, "it is over, and we are defeated." Our faith in God said, "He was in control of the storm, and we will have total victory."

We all could live a life of fulfillment if we chose to change our mindsets. When you make up your mind to live for God and trust His plan, it seems as if all hell breaks loose.

Some of the things He showed me did not even make sense to me, but it is in those times that you must just go along with it.

Giving up can **never be an option**, no matter what you are going through.

"I have cried, kicked, screamed, fallen on my knees, laid out on the floor, and even questioned if I really believed, but I refused to quit." -@KatrinaMarie

Storms do come, but they are never last. Eventually, they will end, and the sun will shine bright again. I am a living testimony of what God can do!

No one must tell me because I have my OWN experience.

✝✝✝

Remember the email stated we would be evicted on October 11, 2017? Well, we made it to November, but now November rent was due. If you're keeping track, rent had not been **paid** since August, but we were still living in our apartment. *Nobody but God could cover us like this. We were surrounded by God's extraordinary grace.*

We received an email from the apartment management stating that if we did not pay the owed amount of $5,476.39 by November 11, 2017, they would start the eviction procedures with the court.

Well, back to the job hunt for me! I was applying everywhere, but no response. This time I was told that I was *over-qualified*. I had 20 years of experience in the food industry and yet could not get a job!

Now I was really starting to feel down, but I knew that would only send me into depression, so I prayed and got myself together because I did NOT want the kids to see me like that.

They were so happy, and I did not want to take that feeling away from them (and every mother know what I'm talking about here).

I know God said His Word could not go out and return void. I know it in my heart.

"So shall my word be that goeth forth out of my mouth: it shall not return unto me void, but it shall accomplish that which I please, and it shall prosper in the thing whereto I sent it." (Isaiah 55:11)

The only thing I had to depend on was my faith. There were so many things telling me to give up, or God will not come through. I had to just stand firm on His Word.

How many apartment rental places do you know of that will allow you to go three months without paying rent?! Generally, after 5 days, they have already filed papers with the court to evict you. We knew God was the only reason we had a roof over our heads still!

†††

This is a faith *journey*. Even though things seemed challenging, we did not want to return to Mississippi. We believed our new life was in Tennessee, and nothing in our spirit told us to return.

REMINDER

Listen to GOD, and not 'man'. Don't even listen to your OWN insecurities. Listen to GOD.

@katrinamarie   #TheEncourager

I knew God had an amazing plan for our lives here, even though we could not see it yet. Mississippi was comfortable for us, but we wanted a change.

Yes, it would make sense for us to return to Mississippi because we had good jobs, money saved, our bills were always paid on time, and we could do amazing things for others.

Paying the bill for us was an afterthought. There was only one problem we were still having in Mississippi…

We were not happy, and we did not experience joy.

We knew there was more to our lives than where we were. I knew there was something God needed me to do. I needed a fresh start or new beginning away from all the distractions surrounding me. I needed to be somewhere I could hear God *clearly*.

"This faith journey was not easy, but I know God is with us every step of the way, and the reward in the end will be greater than the things we faced while on this journey." -@KatrinaMarie

✝✝✝

Sometimes in life, we must get out of our comfort zone. Change is uncomfortable, but it is good for our growth.

We did get some good news. God blessed my husband with his full-time shift! Remember, my husband was only working 3 days a week. God increased him to 5 days a week, with Saturdays and Sundays off. That means an increase in our finances… Praise God!

We also got approved for food subsidy from the State, so we could save money on food!

Truth Moment: *We did not know how to ask for help because we were always the ones helping* *everybody else. It was uncomfortable to humble ourselves in this area, but we did it anyway.*

†††

This peace that I am feeling right now can only come from **trusting God**, and worrying does not do anything but cause stress, depression, and anxiety.

I do not want to live like that when my Father in Heaven has unlimited resources and wants the best for me. I am nowhere near perfect, but I strive daily to live a life pleasing to God and to reflect who He is.

I know whatever happens in our lives, God has an amazing plan, and He loves us unconditionally. He sees the best in us, even when we cannot see it for ourselves.

Katrina Marie
@katrinamarie

And Jesus said unto them, Because of your unbelief: for verily I say unto you, If ye have faith as a grain of mustard seed, ye shall say unto this mountain, Remove hence to yonder place; and it shall remove; and nothing shall be impossible unto you.

#SteppingOutOnFaith
#CanGodConsiderYou

Matthew 17:20
(King James Version)

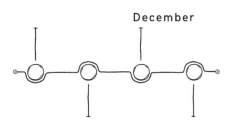

Chapter 3

2017

The Summons

We are still living in our apartment, thanks to God! We spent the Thanksgiving holiday with our family visiting from Mississippi.

I was so looking forward to their visit! The visit almost didn't take place due to some financial hardships my family were facing themselves, but I prayed to my Father, and He made a way... as always! God knew I needed a break and family visiting during Thanksgiving was just what the Doctor ordered.

✝✝✝

My family had no idea we were facing eviction because we had not shared it with *anyone*. And we were not about to share it then. Instead, we enjoyed the delicious southern cooked Thanksgiving meal!

Besides, food is my specialty.

We prepared cornbread dressing, baked chicken, collard greens, honey baked ham, homestyle macaroni and cheese, peach cobbler, and sweet potato pie. The food was delicious!

We were with family and we had a good time laughing, eating, watching movies, and just being in each other's presence.

My sisters and I decided to do the normal tradition after Thanksgiving in America, and shop the "Black Friday sale" on a Thursday night. If you've never shopped in America (especially in the South) during Black Friday, then you will not understand the experience!

Every major outlet do outlandish sales. You can literally buy a 75-inch television for $400 on Black Friday, when the normal price is $2,500 (I'm making the numbers up, but you get my point - crazy discounts worldwide). It is quite an experience that I will share another time.

Anyhow, all of the activities from Black Friday pre-occupied my mind from my family's reality. Rather than focus on our situation, we decided to enjoy the present moment of our family visiting from out of town.

My eldest son, sister-cousin, and goddaughter all visited the day after Thanksgiving. Everybody knows Thanksgiving dinner tastes even better the day after! So you know what we did, we ate leftovers.

The next day, we all went to Nashville, and walked around the city and took pictures. We had an awesome holiday weekend.

✝✝✝

God has really been so, so good to us. He has taken care of us ever since we moved to Tennessee. I am so grateful because there is no way that we could make it without God.

He is a God of His Word. If His Word said it, then He would make good on His Word.

✝✝✝

Well, it was time for our family to leave. I have to say I was kind of sad, but I knew they had to return to their own homes. Thanksgiving was now over, and it was time for us to return to our daily routine.

My husband and I decided to go on a 3-day fast. We really needed guidance and direction from God, and we also needed a miracle. The fast started the Tuesday after Thanksgiving.

We prayed 3 times a day and reframed from eating foods from sunset to sundown. We prayed for strength, wisdom, knowledge, spiritual guidance, family, church, nation, etc. You get the picture. We wanted to see the hand of God working.

Well, it seemed during the fast our situation got worst! I was sitting in my living room studying the Word of God, had just finished praying when I heard a knock at my front door. I went and looked through the peephole, and it was a white man.

My first thought was to not open the door because I did not know who this man was, but my inner me—which was the Holy Spirit—said to open the door. So I did.

I opened the door, and we were being summoned to court by the apartment management. We were sued for $5,476.39 for back pay rent, attorney, and court fees. I politely signed the papers and thanked the deputy.

I was not upset because I knew we owed the money, and they could have evicted us three months ago... the deputy was only doing his job.

I looked at the summons with tears rolling down my face and said, "Lord, I trust you!"

I could not worry about it because I knew we did not have the money, but our Father in Heaven did. I prayed to God and asked for a miracle in our finances to take care of our debts. After I prayed, I went back to studying the Word of God.

REMINDER

I have learned that our Father always does what is best for us even if we feel it is not the best. He sees what we CAN NOT see.

@katrinamarie   #TheEncourager

Now my phone rang and I answered it. It was the company I paid my car note to. They informed me that if I did not make a payment, they were going to repossess my car.

What? First the summons and now the repo? Maybe we should not be fasting because since we started, all sorts of things had been happening.

The lady on the phone from the car dealership asked me if I was working, and I responded 'no'.

She then asked me to confirm my address and phone number, you know, the usual prompts when the bill collectors call.

Now, I could have given her a different address so they could not find my car, but I did not want to be dishonest, so I gave her my address.

For a moment, I thought *'this was all my fault. If I had continued to look for a job, none of this would be happening.'*

I had to quickly rebuke the enemy and say it was not my fault. I surrender my will to the will of God for my life. If God wanted me to have a job, I would have had one by now after submitting over 50 applications.

I had no problem working if God wanted me to do that. I'm not a lazy person. I have worked for over 20 years, so I was no stranger to it. I knew whatever God was doing had a purpose, and He was going to fulfill it. Even though I'm not completely sure where He is taking me, I wanted to make sure I make myself available to Him.

I was trusting the process even though it was hard sometimes, and besides, God never shows us the total journey all at once. He knows we would go a different route or let fear scare us to think we couldn't do it. He wants us to have total faith in Him.

It seemed like the more we prayed, the more the walls started falling. Going back to Mississippi seemed like a good option, but I had to see the journey through.

The enemy is a liar and wanted us to feel like we were defeated and that God had abandoned us. God is our Shepherd and would never leave us. We had to make sure we weren't coming into an agreement with the enemy by continuing to confess the Word of God.

Ephesians Chapter 6: 13-17 tells us:

13 Wherefore take unto you the whole armour of God, that ye may be able to withstand in the evil day, and having done all, to stand.

14 Stand therefore, having your loins girt about with truth, and having on the breastplate of righteousness;

15 And your feet shod with the preparation of the gospel of peace;

16 Above all, taking the shield of faith, wherewith ye shall be able to quench all the fiery darts of the wicked.

17 And take the helmet of salvation, and the sword of the Spirit, which is the Word of God.

This is how we will fight against the enemy's lies. We knew God would rescue us; we just didn't know *when* or *how*.

"Now let me tell you, it was hard, and some days anxiety was getting the best of me, but we continued to pray, study the Word, and kept our eyes on God, so we didn't get stressed out." -@KatrinaMarie

Remember, nobody but my husband and I knew what was going on. Our kids didn't even know. They only knew we didn't have the money we used to have because I wasn't working.

††††

Now let me tell you HOW we were tested with money. Marvin (my husband) and I started receiving checks in the mail from different loan companies. We had to cash the checks, which automatically activated the loan. I received a total of about $8,000.

Now, I know you are probably wondering, 'That's Great! You can use that money and get a place to live."

No Way! I shredded every check. That's Right! I Did!

We trusted in God, remember? We knew God wouldn't put us in more debt than we were already in.

REMINDER

By the way, it doesn't make sense to believe God for debt cancellation, and then add to the debt.

@katrinamarie   #TheEncourager

It didn't take a rocket scientist to figure out that we needed the money desperately, but we chose to trust the plan God had for us.

†††

It was court day, December 7, 2017, and we must be in court by 1:00 p.m. We woke up, studied the Word, prayed, and enjoyed our morning together. For some reason, we weren't afraid. We had peace in our Spirit.

Finally, we headed to court. Upon arrival, we met with the lawyer who represented our case for the Apartment Management. When we entered the hallway, the lawyer conversed with another man. We sat on a bench in front of the lawyer and the other man, waiting our turn.

The lawyer told the man that he had 10 days to move out of his apartment. Turned out, that man was being sued by the same Apartment Management as we were.

My husband and I were just talking while waiting, and I looked up, and the way that man's face pierced me down to my soul. He looked hurt, depressed, and unsure of what to do. He then asked the lawyer if he could have until December 29th to move out, at least his kids would be out of school and enjoy Christmas. The lawyer responded he needed approval from the Apartment Management before he could agree to the man's terms.

I immediately prayed to God that he would show the man favor with his request. The lawyer returned and said they could give him until December 28th, and the man happily agreed. *I was like, "Thank you, Jesus!"*

See, sometimes in life, you need to intercede for others. Everyone's faith level is not the same. Even though we were in the same situation, I prayed for him.

My husband and I were playing and laughing, and this man didn't know what he was going to do. He had kids and a family. I had compassion for him and could believe for him. Well, now it was our turn.

The lawyer went over what we owed and told us also that we had to move in 10 days. My husband asked if we could have the same move-out date as the other man. The Apartment Management said, "YES!" Also, they asked if we could pay $150 a month, starting January 2018, until our balance was paid in full. We agreed. Our date to move out of the apartment was December 28, 2017. Well, that was over!

✝✝✝

"Thank You, God, for divine favor! Yes, we had to move, but God doesn't close one door without opening another." -@KatrinaMarie

Our season at the apartment was up. The situation could have turned out differently. Remember, we hadn't paid rent in five months, and they were only asking that we pay for the five months instead of the 12-month lease. Who would let you live five months somewhere without paying rent for that long?? It was the favor of God on our family. Period.

The uncommon was starting to become standard for us. It was part of God's plan for us.

On the way home, I prayed for the young man in court. My prayer was for God to provide him and his kids somewhere else to stay, and that He would provide them with all of their needs.

I always think about other people regardless of what I'm going through. It's the Spirit of God who lives in me. God is a part of me, and I am a part of Him. He created me to be His servant, and I wanted to ensure I represented Him well.

At this point in our journey, I never thought about getting ready to be homeless. I knew God would supply all of our needs. I was excited about what was next for my family.

See, God is going to take us from glory to glory.

✝✝✝

Time is starting to wind down for us to move. On December 21, 2017, my husband kissed me, told me he loved me and left for work. Moments later, he came back in and said that my car was not outside.

It had been repossessed. I was three months behind on my car note. They were just doing their job.

My husband left for work. My heart was getting heavy because I was starting to feel guilty again. But I kept reminding myself of Who my Father was.

I called my husband, and we prayed together. My husband comforted me and said, "God got us!" He assured me that none of what we were going through was my fault.

How many men would say that? They would have told you to get any job because we got bills to pay.

My husband believed in the plans God had for our family. We truly believed God would deliver us and provide us with a home and financial breakthrough.

Once again, we knew we were in a position for God to perform a miracle in our lives. We would see God in a way we had never seen before.

I called the car dealership so I could get my personal belongings out of the car and to find out how much I needed to pay to get the car back. I mean, I was almost done paying for it. I only owed about $4200, and I wanted my car.

I didn't believe God would allow me to lose my car and I was almost done paying for it, but I also knew if I lost it, then God had something better in store for me.

The dealership told me that if I came up with $1900, I could get my car back. I didn't have it, and besides, we had one week to move out of our apartment.

On top of that, Christmas was in four days, and we hadn't bought the kids anything. I thank God for our children; they hadn't even *asked* for anything. They were excited that they could get a shirt they wanted out of Goodwill.

God blessed us with children who were grateful for whatever they got. They are children of faith. They even kept me encouraged from time to time when my Spirit was down. I knew one day God would give them the desires of their hearts because they believed in what He could do.

Remember, they didn't know we were being evicted. They were going to spend the holidays with our family, so our prayer was that by the time they returned, we would be in our new home.

We know God wouldn't leave us homeless with our kids. He would provide a roof over our heads. He had always taken care of us, and He would continue to do so. All we had was God's Word, our faith, and each other.

Katrina Marie
@katrinamarie

The Lord had said to Abram, "Go from your country, your people and your father's household to the land I will show you…"

#SteppingOutOnFaith
#CanGodConsiderYou

Genesis 12:1
(New International Version)

Chapter 4

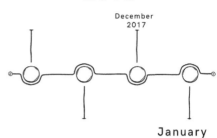

Eviction Time

W e have two days to move now with no money and no place to go. My faith in that moment was in God. I was trusting in His Word. This was the only way I wasn't going to give up.

Remember God is always in control, and He is the Creator of time.

December 28, 2017 was eviction day. Time to move. We woke up and went to the storage place to get a unit. We ended up getting a smaller one for our items like clothes, television, and dishes. That was all we could afford.

We didn't have the money to get a U-Haul to move our furniture. So, after we secured the storage unit, we made several trips using my husband's car to move our personal items.

We donated our deep freezer to our neighbor, and our kids' beds were donated to Goodwill. We cleaned the apartment but had to leave our living room, bedroom set, and washer and dryer behind—we had no way to move them or a place to store them. So we took all that we could.

It was time to go. I began to cry rapidly. I looked around the apartment and thanked God for the five months we were there. We left and went to the front office to turn in the keys.

We went to the hotel and paid for one night because my husband had to be at work Friday morning. I knew check-out was at 11:00 a.m, so I asked for a late check-out because I didn't have anywhere to go until my husband got off at 7:00 p.m.

We prayed and went to bed. We were exhausted from moving all day; on top of that, it was freezing cold as we were in the dead of winter.

We woke up around 5:30 a.m. so I could take my husband to work and I could keep the car. We were down to one car now that mine was repossessed.

Anyway, after taking Marvin to work, I went back to the hotel, enjoyed the free breakfast, and laid down until check out time at 12:00 p.m. After checking out, I went to the library and hung out there until 5:00 p.m.

That's right, I was there for five hours. I had nowhere else to go. It was cold outside, and the Library was warm and had a restroom. Traffic was normally heavy around rush hour time, so I went to a hamburger fast food restaurant to grab a bite to eat, then headed to my husband's job. I made it there around 5:45 p.m.

He was late getting off, so I had to wait in the car until 8:00 p.m. I was cold and tired, but didn't want to sleep in the car due to the area where my husband worked.

My husband was finally off, and I was so glad to see him! Since he was off for the next three days, we decided we would return to Mississippi, where our kids were (they spent the holidays in Mississippi with family).

At least that way, we would have somewhere to stay for the time being, and we wouldn't have to worry about money for a hotel as we can stay with family. So we packed a few things and headed off to Mississippi. The drive is about four hours and we made it there around 11:45 p.m. We were so excited to see our kids and family. For a moment, our minds were taken away from what we had just gone through.

Our kids still don't know what's happening because they had been with my sister-in-law since Christmas.

Let's fast forward to Sunday, December 31, 2017... We went to watch night at a church we used to attend in Memphis, Tennessee. You could feel the presence of God as soon as you walked in the building.

We spent New Year's Eve praising and worshipping God into the New year 2018. Just because we were going through wasn't going to stop us from praising God.

✝✝✝

January 1, 2018, New Years Day was the hardest day of my life. My daughter kept insisting that she wanted to go home. I knew in my heart it was time to tell her. My husband and I took her outside, away from everyone else, and told her about everything. She broke down and began to cry.

I didn't know how to comfort my daughter. I was hurting now that she was hurting. I told her we had to continue to trust God and that we would make it through together. I wasn't prepared for what she told us next.

She told us that she wanted to move back to Mississippi because when we lived in Mississippi, we had everything. She said that we should have never left.

You know what? She was right. When we lived in Mississippi, we had money, our bills were paid before time, we had a nice house, money in our savings account, and we could take care of their needs and wants.

There was only one thing wrong with all of that. We had no peace, were miserable, no joy, and didn't have a relationship with God like we do now.

We were broken and were only existing. I knew there was more to our lives than where we were. I wouldn't trade that for nothing.

After we finished talking to her about God, we asked her not to tell anyone. She dried her face, smiled, and said, "Okay, I trust God." That brought me great joy to hear her say that.

Because we had nowhere to go, I stayed with my kids at my sister-in-law's house until my kids returned to school after the holiday break. And Marvin returned back to Tennessee because he had to work. He talked to his baby brother about what happened, and his brother agreed to let him stay at his place for the week so he could go to work.

I told my sister-in-law the kids weren't ready to go, so I was going to stay, too. That was my way to cover up that we had no home to go back to. We didn't want to tell everyone because we were ashamed and didn't want them to tell us to move back.

REMINDER

Our faith was in God, and we didn't need anyone questioning our faith.

@katrinamarie   #TheEncourager

Besides, God didn't tell us to move back. We had to be obedient to what He had in store for us. We were already hurting and in pain. We didn't need them, making us feel worse by telling us we shouldn't have moved.

I really didn't expect anyone to understand our faith journey and level right now. Naturally, it didn't make sense, but this was a spiritual journey. We knew one day we would see the goodness of the Lord and that all this would be well worth it.

Sometimes I felt my sister-in-law knew something was wrong, but she never said anything. She treated us with so much hospitality. When she bought her something to eat, she treated us as well. She showed us so much love and compassion, and I thank her for that. It made my life easier because the whole time I was there, I was fighting back my tears.

> *"I was a praying sister because this was the only way*
> *I was fighting the battle in my mind."*
> *-@KatrinaMarie*

Focusing on God and listening to praise and worship music kept my mind off our circumstances. I couldn't let our circumstances become bigger than God.

So, let's fast forward to Sunday, January 7, 2018, the day before the kids had to return to school so we had to go back to Mount Juliet, Tennessee. My sister-in-law prepared a big breakfast, we showered and packed up everything in the car to leave. My husband drove down to pick us up and take us back to Mount Juliet. We stopped for gas and snacks for the kids and hit the road.

Now while we were on our way back, we finally told our son about everything that happened. His eyes filled up with water. The tears began to flow frequently. We told him that it was okay for him to cry. We told him we would still take him to see his friends with whom he built a relationship. We also told him that God would take care of us. We just had to continue to believe as a family and stick together.

I looked back at my daughter and asked her if she was okay, and she smiled back at me and nodded yes while eating her snacks. We finally made it back to Mount Juliet, and stopped by the storage unit so the kids could pick out clothes for school. We ended up paying for a week's stay at an extended hotel in Lebanon, Tennessee. It had a mini condo setting—a stove, refrigerator, television, and cabinet space for food. It also had a washer and dryer to do laundry.

It was a roof over our heads. This was our resting place until God says otherwise. With one car, kids in school and a husband who worked unusual hours, we had to have a strategy on how to operate in our new normal, knowing it was only for a season.

Our daily routine was to wake up at 3 a.m. and take my husband to work; go back to the hotel, lay down until 6 a.m., and then get the kids up and take them to school. I would drop them off at the old apartment complex so

they could still ride the bus with their friends—trying to maintain some type of normalcy for our kids. We knew this was hard for them just as much as it was for us.

Once I dropped them off at school, I would go to the library and put in some job applications. After leaving the library, I would return to the hotel, read my Bible, talk to God, and rest until it was time to pick the kids up from school at 2:45 p.m., and then my husband at 5 p.m. This was our daily routine.

†††

Having only one car caused us to use a lot of gas due to the daily trips we had to make. Living in an Extended Stay Hotel was expensive. It cost almost $500 a week for two beds. Our room was paid for until January 12, 2018. We had no extra money, and we didn't know what was going to happen after that.

We stayed in constant prayer, asking God for help. Sometimes I felt He wasn't even listening or was just silent.

Did God hear my prayers? Of course, He did! So why hadn't He rescued my family yet?

Sometimes in life, we have so much noise around us that it drowns out the small, still voice of God speaking to us. God is always speaking, but we're too busy moving that we don't hear.

"Sometimes we just must BE STILL." -@KatrinaMarie

No situation is too hard for God because He is all-powerful. He is our Creator, and nothing ever catches Him by surprise. Our timing is not God's timing but just know His timing is always on time. His thoughts are not our thoughts, and His plans are not ours. God must get the glory from our life trials. We must learn how to walk by faith and not by sight.

My family was going through some pain, but giving up wasn't an option. We will continue to have faith and keep moving forward.

✝✝✝

Now, believe me when I say this wasn't a walk in the park! My faith had never been tested that hard. I was on edge. I was like a time bomb, ready to explode. The only thing that kept bringing me back was Holy Spirit reminding me of God's Word and going into praise and worship mode.

I was anointed and appointed for this, and I wasn't going to fail. Sometimes the pain can get so intense you just want to give up and return to where you were most comfortable. How could I ever give up on the One who gave me a second chance at life? I couldn't!

With tears running down my face, I said, "I Trust You, Lord!" I couldn't go back. I knew God had so much more for me to do here. Yes, I am uncomfortable, but I won't stop until I receive all God has for my family and me. Whatever it was, I wasn't going to miss it. So, we continued our new daily routine. Together, as a family working as one unit, by God's grace.

†††

One day I applied for a patient care assistant job. After reading their qualifications, I didn't qualify. Something told me to apply anyway because I loved helping people. By the time I returned to the hotel, I had received an email from the job. They invited me for an interview on January 11, 2018, at 10:00 a.m.—which was the next day.

On the day of the interview, we had to limit the number of trips we made to save up gas for me to go to my interview. So my husband went with me to drop off the kids, then we parked in the library parking lot until time for my interview.

We sat in the car, reading our bible plans and discussing what God's Word was saying to us. Anytime we get to talking about God, time flies by. We looked at the time, and it was 9:00 a.m. We had been talking in the library's parking lot since 8:00 a.m. We left and went for my interview.

✝✝✝

We arrived and the interviewer greeted me and asked me to have a seat. What I loved about her was when she was ready to interview me, she came and sat next to me, which made me feel much more comfortable. Most interviewers sit in front of you.

So, she asked if I had experience as a care provider. I explained I didn't have care provider experience per se, but I worked with people for over 20 years and was willing to learn. I told her I always had a servant's heart and loved to help and encourage people.

Giving people hope and lifting their spirits is a part of who I am. This brings me great joy that I can make someone's day.

Let me just say there were no more questions. She said they were looking for people with that kind of spirit and told me I was hired. Thank you, Jesus! I finally had a job.

I didn't get the job I wanted that I was well qualified for, but for a job I wasn't qualified for and had no experience, I was hired on the spot.

See, it's okay to have degrees, certifications, and experiences to qualify for what you want, but don't think that makes you better than someone who doesn't have those because, at the end of the day, God is the One who qualifies us.

REMINDER

It is God Who opens and closes doors. He qualifies me.

@katrinamarie   #TheEncourager

I'm so glad my life is in God's hands instead of man's. Now don't use this as an excuse to NOT put in the work because faith and works go hand in hand.

I was excited and sad at the same time because I received a job after losing everything, but I had to believe it was all part of God's plan.

We left the interview and went back to the hotel. We were really pushing it because our gas was getting low. Praise God! We made it.

My husband and I prayed, talked, and enjoyed lunch. We believed God would bless us with a financial breakthrough because we needed gas to pick up the kids from the bus stop. Time was getting near to pick them up and we had no gas. But we believed in God for a miracle.

†††

It's now 3:45 p.m., and we need to pick up the kids. My husband then remembered he had put his tithes away in his wallet, so he used some of it to get gas.

Now let me tell you, this broke him down because he didn't want God to think he didn't trust in Him. He had never done that before and was upset that he had to, especially when believing and trusting God.

My husband felt like God abandoned him and hadn't heard his prayers. He also used some of the money to pay for two more days in the hotel. I was hurt because I wanted to keep our faith in God. We were going through a rough time, but we had to keep our focus on God and not on our circumstances.

I had to be strong for my family. There was no room for me to be down too. I couldn't allow the enemy to break my family, so I went into immediate prayer. I came against all plots, plans, tricks, and schemes of the enemy.

I sabotaged all his strategies and sent that confusion back to the enemy's camp in the Name of Jesus. Satan, you are a liar and deceiver, and you will do anything to try and make us lose faith in our Heavenly Father. Your plans will not work, and I command you to leave my family alone. For me and my house, we will serve the Lord.

I made sure to pray for my husband and children as well. I had to keep my family covered and on one accord. I understood why my husband did what he did because he knew he was the head of our household, and it was his job to take care of our family. I believed God honored that. Period.

It was not about the money but what was in Marvin's heart. I assured my husband he was our provider, but God is the Ultimate Source of everything we need. We are just stewards over what He has given us. I believed in my heart that it was only the Holy Spirit that even reminded Marvin that he had the money in his wallet.

"I believe our family is our first ministry, and we must take care of our house before we take care of someone else's." -@KatrinaMarie

All this took place in the car while going to pick up the kids from the bus stop, then back to the hotel. As time passed, my husband and I left so I could get to choir practice.

Singing in the choir was a part of my life. I loved praise and worship. Being in the presence of God takes you to a place where you have no worries. And going to choir practice was what I really needed.

One of the songs we learned was *Big*. That song ministered to my soul. My God is big, so strong, and so mighty. God is bigger than anything we could ever go through.

The other song was *God is Preparing Me*. God was on a roll tonight and ministered to me through dance and song!

Everything my family was going through was preparing us for something greater. God had a master plan for us; we just needed His strength to make it through.

†††

Fast forward to Sunday, January 14, 2018, it was time for us to check-out of the Extended Stay hotel. We didn't know what we were going to do. We just prayed about it and headed to church. We were anxious to get there because we needed a Word from God to encourage us.

The church was so awesome! Praise and worship was on another level. I was high off the Holy Spirit. Nothing at that moment mattered to me. I was just happy to be in the house of the Lord.

The message from the Pastor was *When Quitting Looks Attractive*. This message went along with what we were going through. There were many times we wanted to throw in the towel.

We felt all alone. Where is God?

Our lives weren't matching up with His Word.

Why hasn't God answered our prayers? It would have been okay if it was just me and my husband, but we had children.

We couldn't sleep in the car because the temperature was too cold. Even though we thought about quitting, we couldn't do it. All I could think was Jesus never quit on us, so we couldn't quit on Him.

What if Jesus said He couldn't die for someone who didn't deserve it, and came down off the cross? We would still be sinners and sacrifice animals for the sins we committed. We wouldn't be redeemed or have salvation. More importantly, we wouldn't have access to our Heavenly Father.

I'm so grateful for the sacrifice Jesus made for me. That's why I must keep pushing no matter what happens in my life. Despite our natural circumstances, we had to keep our minds focused on God. *That is the only thing that kept us from sinking.*

†††

After service, we went to the mall because we had nowhere to go. While there, I reached out to my family for help. They didn't know what we were going through because I still hadn't told them. I needed money to help purchase my work uniforms.

I called my Madea, and she told me she didn't have it, so she told me to ask my big sister. I called and talked to my big sister, and she told me I should have asked earlier because she had already gone to the grocery store.

I then called my baby sister, and she said she could help me and that what she had to do could wait. She sent me $100.

I was so grateful. "Thank you so much, Sis," is what I told her!

My husband said we needed to leave the mall because it was getting late. We headed back to Mount Juliet. We drove around a while. My husband asked me what we were going to do. I reached out to a friend who lived in the area I met while working at the Casino, and asked if she knew of any shelter for families. She said she couldn't find anything, so we just sat in the parking lot at Walmart.

After a while, my husband finally said we needed to move because the police kept riding in surveillance. The only money we had was the money my baby sister gave me for my work uniforms. I just knew God was going to provide us somewhere to stay.

Philippians 4:19 says, "But my God shall supply all your need according to His riches in glory by Christ Jesus."

Having a roof over our heads was a NEED. *So, God, where are You?*

> *"I was constantly telling my husband and children God would provide. He got our backs."*
> *-@KatrinaMarie*

My family probably looked at me crazy because they saw no evidence. I mean, they could hear me talking, but couldn't see anything happening.

~

Well, we didn't sleep in the car. We took the money my baby sister gave me for work uniforms and got a hotel room. The money paid for one night. And I still found some work uniforms from Goodwill, so it all worked out.

~

I got up early the next morning to take my husband to work, so the kids and I could keep the car. We got a late check-out because we still had no place to go. After dropping off Marvin, I went back to the hotel and got back in bed. I was exhausted from being at the mall and in the car all day.

Even though we were homeless, we were STILL blessed to have a car, my husband was STILL able to go to work, my kids DIDN'T miss school, and we ALWAYS had food to eat.

✝✝✝

I woke the kids up so they could eat the free hotel breakfast. That way, we didn't have to buy food for breakfast. After breakfast, we showered and got dressed. We watched a little TV before we checked out of the hotel.

We packed our clothes, put them back in the car, and checked out. The kids wanted to go to the library, so we headed in that direction. When we got there, it was closed. We forgot that it was Martin Luther King's holiday.

Despite our circumstances, the kids and I found joy in singing songs along with the radio. To see them smile brought joy to my heart. We were all in this together.

Whatever God was doing in our family must be mine blowing because we were really going through!

My phone rang, and it was my friend I met at the Casino who lived in Mount Juliet. She asked me to meet her at Kroger grocery store. She filled our car up with gas and gave me $20 to get the kids some lunch.

I was so grateful to God for allowing her to be so compassionate to us. She knew me, but not my family, but that didn't matter to her. She was concerned about our well-being and just wanted to help.

I believe God allowed me to cross paths with her at the Casino years before because He knew we would cross paths later. I called these 'divine connections.'

I stopped at a fast food restaurant to get the kids something to eat, then headed to our favorite place... that's right! The Mall.

We hung out until it was time to pick my husband up from work. I was praying that God was going to perform a miracle and we would have somewhere to live. *And soon, Lord!*

✝✝✝

I called several churches to see if there were any shelters in our area, and it wasn't. One church gave me a homeless hot-line number. So, I called it, and they told me about low-income apartments, but the waiting list was very long. Some people had already been on the list for over a year.

The lady on the homeless hot-line number gave me a shelter that was near where we used to live, but my family would have to separate. My husband and son would have to stay at one location, and my daughter and I at another. We didn't want to be separated like that, especially with the kids.

I didn't know what else to do because I had never been homeless.

I know you're asking again, *why didn't we go back home to Mississippi?*

We knew God brought us here for a reason. He wouldn't have opened the door if we weren't supposed to be here, and God didn't tell us to go back. God told us to trust Him.

✝✝✝

My husband finally broke down and asked his baby brother for help. His brother paid for one week's stay at another Extended Stay hotel. I thanked his brother because I was just so glad the kids had one week in a stable place.

I woke up the following day and got on my prayer call. It blessed me! You see, I maintained as much of my normal life as I could as far as serving God. So I still attended my prayer calls faithfully.

God was saying, "You keep praying to Me about the same things. I heard you the first time you prayed. Your prayers are being answered, but not in the way you think. Start thanking Me as if you have received everything you asked for. *That's* faith."

REMINDER

Sometimes we get used to how God brought us out before, and we are expecting Him to do it the same way. We must be open to however God blesses us.

@katrinamarie   #TheEncourager

However He blesses us, it will be best. Besides, a Father always wants what's best for His children. I know I do as a mother.

✝✝✝

So, I started my new job as a Patient Care Assistant while we were at the Extended Stay. I worked Monday thru Friday. I had two clients a week. I made $9 an hour for the client I worked 3 days for and $10 an hour for the client I worked 2 days for.

I loved being a PCA because it allowed me to help someone who couldn't help themselves, share the love of Jesus and encourage them. Seeing my clients made me realize that some people are going through some things worse than you. I mean, I was only having problems with an eviction, and here is one of my clients who was confined to a bed, couldn't give herself a bath or go to the restroom on her own, and my other client had a bone disease that left her in constant pain daily.

So, see, I really had nothing to complain about because I really can't say I know how they felt or what they were going through because I have never been in that kind of situation. It makes you learn to be thankful for the things you have and can do and not focus on what you don't have and what you are not able to do. I loved my clients.

Being able to help them with things they couldn't do for themselves was uplifting for me. One of the things I noticed about them is that I never heard them complain about their disabilities. Instead, they focused on the things that they could do and put all their time and energy into that. Now that was a wake-up call to me.

Okay, Holy Spirit, I hear You talking to me. I have learned that every assignment that the Most High has given me was also a lesson for me. I was focusing so much on the problem instead of the problem solver. We must learn to find joy in our situation because, at the end of the day, we already know we have the victory.

Well, I was working now, so everything should be okay, but it wasn't. I never told my family about our situation, so I finally called my Madea and told her all that happened and the reason I didn't say anything. I told her I didn't want to hear we should have stayed in Mississippi and never moved. Madea told me she would have never said that and that she believed God moved us here. She encouraged me and told me everything was going to be okay. I felt relieved because I had finally told her.

Then I reached out to my sister Jamie and shared with her, and we both were going through similar things. God had a plan for us, but we didn't see it right away. We cried together, prayed, and encouraged each other.

I love my sister Jamie so much. She always understood me. She made me embrace who I was and never change myself for anyone. I learned that I am different, and I don't have to apologize to anyone about it. The Most High made me this way, and He never makes mistakes. I *am fearfully and wonderfully made.*

Lastly, I called my sister/cousin Vanessa, and she was shocked. She told me I should have said something, but I had to explain that I had to wait for God to tell me to share. She also gave me some encouraging words and said that if we needed anything, just let her know and that her door was always open to us. I thanked her and told her God didn't tell us to move back.

Now that I have shared my journey with those who God gave me, I felt peace. I told my husband I shared with them, and then he shared with the rest of his family.

Now my husband's older brother was upset with him because they are close, and he told us that he could have helped. My brother-in-law came through for us a lot, and we appreciate him much. I call him 'ballpark', and he calls me 'butterball.' That's the relationship we have with each other. You know when you are feeling down, you don't need anyone kicking you down even further. You need some cheerleaders to tell you, *you got this*.

✝✝✝

The Most High has trained you for this time. We always talk the talk; now it's time to walk the walk. After telling everyone about our situation, we were no longer ashamed about what we were experiencing because when it was all over, we knew God would show himself strong and mighty and get all the glory.

The more people that knew, the more God got the glory. When you are in a storm of this magnitude, you need people in your life that will continue to have faith with you, pray with you, and encourage you when you feel like giving up. It didn't matter what people were saying behind our backs because we knew that The Most High would elevate us right before their eyes.

"God would make sure our enemies would know that He was with us." -@KatrinaMarie

Katrina Marie
@katrinamarie

Many are the afflictions of the righteous: but the Lord delivereth him out of them all.

#SteppingOutOnFaith
#CanGodConsiderYou

Psalm 34:19
(King James Version)

Chapter 5

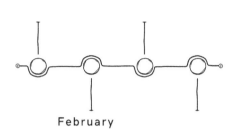

February

The Church

Our week's stay was up at the Extended Stay Hotel, and, yet again, we had nowhere else to go. We ended up sleeping in the car in the hotel's parking lot.

I was so hurt. I felt like God had abandoned us. God seemed silent in our lives.

We just prayed, and Holy Spirit brought back to my remembrance of the homeless hotline. We called a while ago and they gave us a contact called, Passion Hands.

I didn't want my family to be separated, but I would do anything to prevent my kids from sleeping in the car again. I cried for the majority of the night.

My husband comforted me the best way he knew how. He told me to get some sleep and it would be okay. The next day, I dropped my husband off at work and took the kids to the storage unit so they could get dressed for school.

Then we went to Walmart so we could wash our faces and brush our teeth. I dropped the kids at school and went to work myself. Once I got off work, I swallowed my pride and called the Nazarene Church in Lebanon, which was hosting the homeless shelters.

I called, and no one answered, so I left a voicemail. Later, my phone rang. It was Pastor Sam from the Nazarene Church.

Pastor Sam greeted me and politely asked how he could help. I explained my situation, and he told me he had a place to sleep, but we would have to be separated. I told him that wouldn't be a problem. He told me to be at the Nazarene Church at 5:30 p.m. and ask for Regan.

†††

So, after I picked the kids up from school, I headed to the church. When we arrived, we asked for Regan. We introduced ourselves, and then we met Pastor Sam. He told me they had never had a family come to the church needing a place to stay.

He was honest and said that he didn't know what to do with us. Because we had kids, he didn't want to separate us (remember my prayer earlier?). The church fed the community, so we ate while Pastor Sam devised a plan for our family.

So, Pastor Sam told me they had an empty storage room at the church, and we could stay there until he could come up with something else.

The church also housed students who attended a practical ministry school. Pastor Sam introduced us to

The Church's parking lot

Karen, one of the head students, and told us she would be our point of contact. The church had a washer and dryer, showers, and a full kitchen. It had everything we needed!

I was so grateful to The Most High for keeping our family together. I don't know what God was doing, but I knew it would make sense one day.

I told them I had to leave and pick my husband up from work, so Pastor Sam assured me it would be okay to leave the kids with Karen, and he also introduced me to the church security, Jack.

Jack always looked out for the church and the people, so I left to pick my husband up from work. After I told him all that had happened, he was relieved that we had a place to sleep together.

†††

Once again, we were in a new place, that also needed a new daily routine. We still only had one car, but at least we weren't sleeping in it.

Our new 'new' normal looked something like this: Woke up early to drop husband at work and kids at school, then off to work I went. After I got off work, I picked the kids up from school—oh I forgot to mention, my kids went to two different schools; one was in middle school while the other was a high schooler. So I after I picked the kids, I picked up my husband from work, then headed back to the church to eat dinner, which was served at 5:00 p.m.

†††

I worked as a Patient Care Assistant until the kids were released from school for their summer break. After that, I had to put in my notice because I wasn't allowed to leave them at the church without a guardian.

We moved to the church on February 19, 2018, and it was now June 2018. Pastor Sam wanted to meet with us and develop a plan for us to live there. The offer Pastor Sam came up with was that I would cook in the kitchen three days a week in exchange for room and board for my family. Of course, this was only temporary until we found our own place.

The church had a need for a cook, I had the experience and we also had a need for a place to stay. I agreed because we had nowhere else to go, and all the years of experience working in the food industry gave me an upper hand.

†††

The church was a Nazarene Church, so periodically, we attended their bible classes. It was different from the traditional Baptist churches we attended, but let me tell you, the presence of God could truly be felt.

At first, we were uncomfortable because most of the church was white, and we were Black; but they didn't look at our color; they looked at our needs and wanted to help. They showed the love of Jesus. They didn't just talk about it; they lived it.

We found out that the church was very well-known in the community. They fed the homeless and community seven days a week. They had a program for homeless men and women released from jail who had a drug or alcohol addiction or simply needed healing or deliverance. They focused on sharing Jesus in their program because they knew this was the only way they could walk in freedom by accepting Jesus as their Lord and Savior. They let them know that no matter what they have done or been through, they were loved by God and could be saved.

✝✝✝

Working in the kitchen allowed me to meet and talk to several people in the program. Their stories brought me to tears. What we were experiencing had nothing on what they had gone through. I used my skills to serve fine-dining to let them know they were loved and deserved the best. Besides, they are people too.

So often, people look at the homeless, drug addicts, and alcoholics and start passing judgment when we are all one second away from losing it all. We all have different ways we cope with trauma or experiences we deal with in life. We never take the time to ask them to tell us their story.

REMINDER

We all have a story. The question is: are you BRAVE enough to tell it?

@katrinamarie   #TheEncourager

Most of the homeless that we met had good jobs. That's right! As one of my friends, Chef K, would say, "We are the working homeless."

I never heard of that. How could you be working and homeless? Most made too much for low-income housing or made too little for the market price. There was nothing in-between.

*The room in the church where our family
slept for over a year*

I mean, we had an eviction that kept us from renting. We had an excellent rental history for years, but that didn't matter. They were only focused on our *now*. What happened to showing mercy and grace?

> *"Life happens sometimes; that's why we must keep our eyes focused on God and keep our faith in Him."*
> *-@KatrinaMarie*

I enjoyed working in the kitchen, but it became more than I could handle, so God sent me Grace for help. That's right! My new friend, Grace, showed up and worked in the kitchen with me.

Grace was just what I needed. We grew so close. We would go for a 3-mile walk in the park before kitchen duty. It gave us time to share and reflect on God. It was our therapy session. She helped me, and I helped her. We were what each other needed.

God knows how to set up divine connections.

✝✝✝

Every day we fixed a 5-course meal. We had meat, starch, a vegetable, salad, and dessert. Grace was excellent at making desserts. I told her that was her gift and she needed to sell them. Well, today, she bakes cakes as another stream of income. I digress, back to the story...

To stay ahead of the game in the kitchen, I planned the menu for the entire week, and then Grace and I would prep to stay ahead. We ran the kitchen like a restaurant, which was how we managed everything.

Food was donated 3 days a week, so we had to ensure the food lasted. First in, first out was the motto, and if it wasn't any good, we threw it away. On Thursdays and Sundays, another group came in to serve, so I was off those days. Did you catch that? I went from cooking 3 days a week (per our original agreement) to 5 days a week!

The kitchen had quickly become a full-time job, and that wasn't the agreement with Pastor Sam. I didn't say anything because of all the smiles I saw when people were eating... *Maybe this was all part of God's plan.*

✝✝✝

We used to hear all the time how our kids just lit up the church. They stated how polite and respectful my children were and that they always volunteered to help. Well, we did our best to bring our children up in the Lord because we knew there was no way they would make it in this world without Him.

They were able to attend several youth camps and experience Holy Spirit. They also decided to accept Jesus as their Lord and Savior and get baptized.

My husband and kids also helped out in the kitchen and enjoyed talking with everyone and helping serve. Everyone said my family brought joy to their lives.

Marvin would sit down and eat with the men. It allowed him to speak in their lives and, as we say, meet them where they are. Marvin built relationships with the men there. We were intentional about remembering everyone's name. They would just light up when we called them by name. It made them feel they weren't invisible, and they existed. *Miracles were happening before our eyes, and I'm glad we got to be a part of it.*

We struggled financially because my husband was the only one working as time passed. We continued to apply for places to stay but kept hearing, 'No!' We started trying to buy a home but kept getting the same response, 'No!' We heard 'no' so much that it no longer bothered us. We became numb to it. We kept applying and kept looking for our home.

Instead of "no", we heard, "not here" or "not you".

My husband had a house in his name back in Mississippi that his mom was living in, and she had been late on the mortgage, which was why they wouldn't allow us to buy. She had been living there for about 12 years at the time.

Instead of being upset, we prayed for my mother-in-law because we felt that was God's way of letting us know she was having financial difficulties. Had it not been for us trying to buy a home in Tennessee, we probably wouldn't have known she needed help. They say God works in mysterious ways.

Anyhow, the mortgage people told us that we needed to wait one year and not miss a mortgage payment at all, before we could apply for a new home. Worrying and crying weren't going to do anything, so we kept moving.

✝✝✝

Well, summer was almost over, and it's time for the kids to return to school. It was July 26, 2018, and God showed up and showed out! God sent a woman I helped a week before in the kitchen to be a blessing to our family. We called her our 'Angel'. She bought school clothes for Shiya and Trell, school supplies, stuff for me and my husband, a $100 gas card, a $100 Walmart gift card, and a $100 Burkes Outlet gift card .

The only thing I could do was cry because God came through for my family in such a major way by using this young lady. She said God put it on her heart to help our family because we were in need. She shared with us that her husband died prematurely, and always wanted to give back and help someone in need.

When I thanked her, she said it was all God. How could someone who doesn't know you tell you they love and care about your well-being? It's all because Jesus lives in them. ***Jesus is so real, and He has revealed Himself to us daily.***

I was overwhelmed by the blessings God had given us that day, and deep down in my heart, I knew He was not done. He blessed us every day that week. I was so excited about what God had in store for us.

Lord, I am so grateful, and thank You for being our Provider.

I learned that we are God's instruments in the earth's realm. He uses us to be the answers to someone's prayers. Will you obey His instructions, even when you don't understand?

✝✝✝

My life was so busy that I needed a pause. I remembered I was invited to a paint brunch at the women's house, so I decided to go. Wow, I really enjoyed myself! It felt good getting away from the church and hanging out with friends.

We painted a dragonfly. We were outside. There was a breeze, the birds were chirping, a rooster was crowing, and the bees were buzzing. The sounds of nature were so peaceful. The perfect setting to paint. It was very therapeutic, and I wanted to continue painting because it took my mind off the things that were going on, and I just focused on my paintbrush stroking back and forth on the canvas.

I even chose colors that looked peaceful to me. Purple for royalty and my favorite color; yellow for light; turquoise reminded me of the water at the beach; white reminded me of being pure and clean; and pink for sweet-smelling roses. I threw the silver in just to enhance the painting.

I must say I did a great job for a non-artist, but when you are painting from your heart, that's all that matters. My painting looked the way I felt.

Thank you, Joann, for inviting me! You knew exactly what I needed! Joann was the manager in charge of the women's house. She was a sweet soul; every time I saw her, she often told me she was praying for my family. My family was surrounded by prayers constantly.

Artwork by Katrina Marie

Thank you, Lord, for such an amazing day! My Spirit was rejuvenated.

✝✝✝

We were still living in the church, and I was working in the kitchen. I knew if we were ever going to get that eviction paid off, I needed to get a job. I kept talking to Pastor Sam about getting a job because that was the only way we could get the eviction paid off and get our own place. The agreement of me working in the kitchen in return for my family having a place to stay made me feel torn between my family having a place to live and getting a job.

If I got a job, we would have to leave the church because the agreement would be broken. I was like, *Lord, how does Pastor Sam expect us to get our own place if I wasn't working?* Marvin was working, but his income alone couldn't take care of all of our debt and recurring bills.

I prayed about it and left it alone.

✝✝✝

My brother-in-law sent me a text message about an insurance company hiring. I looked at that as a sign from God. I applied for the job, went on the interview and was offered the job the same day!

I was offered $17 an hour working from 11:00 a.m. to 7:00 p.m., starting December 4, 2018. I knew that time would be difficult with only one car, but I accepted the job anyway and told God what I needed to perform the job.

Well, we went to bible class that night, and afterwards, Pastor Sam said he needed to talk to me. He offered for he and Passion Hands to pay me to work in the kitchen. I told him I had already accepted a job offer from the insurance company. He then asked if we had found a place to stay, and, of course we had not.

I just kept praying and trusting God for guidance. I knew anytime one door closed, God always opened another. I wasn't going to let anyone make me feel like I didn't have any other options because God never ran out of options.

We must trust the plan and process God has for us.

†††

The church had what they called *Thursday Night Fire* service, and my friend, Grace invited me. That night changed my life.

My new friends, Chad and Brooke, were the leaders for that particular night. Chad saw me crying and came and whispered in my ear. Take it this man didn't know me at all but was able to tell me things about me only God could have shown him.

After he whispered in my ear, I just lost it. I ended up going through deliverance with him and his wife that night, and the pain and weight I had on me were lifted.

"I have been free ever since!" -@KatrinaMarie

See, before that night, I was broken, abused, confused, weak, bleeding inside, a people pleaser, and constantly worried about what people thought of me.

I wore a mask for so long that I lost who I truly was. I was tired of living a lie and wanted to be healed and delivered.

REMINDER

The more I prayed and sought God about healing, the more He showed me healing was already mine. I had to receive it.

@katrinamarie   #TheEncourager

Once again, God will have you at the right place and time. I believe in divine connections. I thank the Most High for bringing these wonderful souls into my life. Now I am walking in the power and authority He gave me. I am finally free!

It took some time to get here, but I made it.

I'm different now, and I embrace it because God made me this way. I am not who the world says I am, but who my Father in heaven says I am.

People will always try to bring up your past, but once you have been washed by the Blood of the Lamb, you are cleansed.

Romans 8:1 says, "There is therefore now no condemnation to them which are in Christ Jesus, who walk not after the flesh, but after the Spirit."

If you are ready to walk in this kind of freedom, all you must do is just say, "I surrender, Lord."

All it takes is your YES! *-Katrina Marie*

After that amazing Thursday night service, I began to attend Chad and Brooke's bible training school. I donated $5 because I couldn't afford the full tuition; but I must tell you that it was a breath of fresh air! To sit at the feet of Jesus and be saturated in His Word, and to do so freely without anyone looking at you strange, was amazing.

The whole atmosphere was an atmosphere of worship, and I loved it there. Everyone had the same desire. They wanted to be saturated in the presence of God. I felt it was where I belonged. They take the Word piece by piece and break it down slowly so you can understand. There was no rush. They allowed Holy Spirit to take control and have His way. Everyone was on one accord.

They accepted me in without any strings attached. They loved me for who I was and I didn't have to change. That was an amazing feeling! They prayed for my family constantly, and our relationship grew over time.

I don't know what God was up to, but He allowed my family to meet some fantastic people along the faith journey. I'm excited to see what He has in store next!

✝✝✝

Well, it's getting close to starting my new job, and I still hadn't figured out the car situation. Yet, we were headed to church anyway. We didn't stop going to church just because things were a little tight.

Service was good as always. Now I never shared with my pastor about our situation. So, when he asked if anyone needed prayer, I stayed behind. I felt it was time to share with my pastor. When it was my turn for prayer, and He asked what I needed prayer for, I whispered in his ear that my family had been evicted from our apartment and was living in a church, and I wanted God to bless us with our own home. He prayed for my family and then told me to call the church to set up a meeting with him.

Well, I did just that and went to meet with my pastor. He asked me to tell him what was happening, and I did. He told me sometimes we go through things longer because we don't ask for help. He put me in contact with someone he knew, which was one of the principals at my children's school. The school didn't know what we were going through either because I was afraid they would take my children away from me, and I didn't want that to happen. I even used someone else's address to register them for school.

The principal reached out to me, and I explained our situation to her. She put us in contact with a lady named Ashley. Ashley was another angel God brought into our lives. Ashley called me, and I told her our story. She sent a bus to pick my children up from the church in the morning for school. Mind you, the church was not in my kid's school zone. *Can I say nothing but the favor of God?* Ashley also gave us food and gas cards to help with all of the back-and-forth driving we were doing.

God just kept showing out. He was our Provider, and I thank Him for it!

†††

December 4, 2018—my first day of training at the insurance company. Working in a call center was something I had never done, but I thought if God opened the door for me, He would give me what I needed to be successful.

The training was kind of hard because it was so much information to digest. It gave me anxiety, and I was starting to feel I couldn't do it because I failed my test. Finally, one of the younger girls told me I was overthinking it and to just relax.

I asked the Holy Spirit for wisdom and understanding of all this auto insurance terminology. Holy Spirit answered my prayers, and I passed the rest of my test and graduated from the class. Training went by fast, and it was time for me to work the scheduled 11am -7pm. I ended up working this schedule for only one week.

Turned out, a young man overhead me discussing with another staff member that I may have to quit because of the hours. Well, he later approached me and offered to switch hours with me! His shift was.... Wait for it... 8:00 a.m. - 5:00 p.m. Just like that.

Another prayer answered!

Once I got off work, I told my husband, Marvin, what happened, and he said he wanted to sow a seed in that young man's life for helping us. My husband gave him a thank you card with a $100 bill.

Wow! Look at God! He showed up and out again. Can I tell you again, divine connections? God has people out here just for you. They are a part of your destiny and the answer to your prayers.

✝✝✝

Our angel friend called and said a family wanted to adopt my family for Christmas—and she wanted to ask the kids what they wanted.

During this whole journey, my kids never complained about anything. They had faith as well that God was going to bless us. God made sure that they were taken care of. He showed them during this faith journey that He is a Living God, and they could witness His power right before their eyes.

The school also reached out to me and wanted me to ask them what they wanted for Christmas. So, let's just say that God blew their minds. They had so many presents that it took a while to open all their gifts!

I stood there amazed at how God had provided for them. Tears began to fall from my eyes because I was so grateful that He had showered the kids with so much.

The Brown family witnessed first hand what Ephesians 3:20 says, *"Now unto Him that is able to do exceeding abundantly above all that we ask or think, according to the power that worketh in us."*

My Father came through for His children. My children have always been grateful for what they had and never asked for much, and I believe in my heart that God rewarded them for their faithfulness and humbleness.

Sometimes when I was down, my kids would encourage me and tell me God got us and things weren't as bad as they seemed. They would ask me to stop crying so much.

They were right. We were all together, and that was all that mattered.

My other surprise was that my eldest son, Frazier, came to visit us from Mississippi. I was so happy to see him because we missed him so much. He stayed at the church with us for a week and didn't want to leave. He thought it was cool and fun to be living in a church.

I guess it depends on your perception!

He loved the idea that he had full access to the altar when he wanted to. I never even looked at it that way.

✝✝✝

The previous cook returned to the kitchen with the help of a few volunteers. Some of the people were sad because I was no longer cooking, but I explained to them that I had a job and that I needed to make money to help my husband get us a place to stay.

That's what I thought. If I got a job, then we could get a home faster. But we were still living in the church, and I knew because I was no longer cooking, they would eventually ask us to leave. Thankfully, the church allowed us to stay longer.

✝✝✝

It's January 2019, and we survived yet another year. I was so grateful to my Heavenly Father for keeping us. Everything seemed to be going well. My kids were staying with friends occasionally, hanging out, and having fun. My new job was going well, and I had mastered being a call center customer representative, even though some days were stressful.

We had been living at the church for over a year. At first, it was strange, but we learned to celebrate where we were because we knew it was only temporary. One day after bible class, Pastor Sam invited Marvin and me over to hang out at his house that weekend. We were also invited to a bonfire at my friend Grace's house that night.

The kids had a football game, so we dropped them off at their school and headed to Pastor Sam's house. We hung out and laughed and talked a bit, and then Marvin had to leave to pick up the kids.

Pastor Sam then asked if we had found any place to stay, and I said no. I told him we still were working on getting the eviction paid off. He then dropped the bomb on me. He stated he didn't know how to tell us that we had to leave the church. He said what was supposed to be a couple weeks turned into over a year. He was supposed to tell us a month ago that we had to leave but didn't know how because we were like family.

He told us we had until March 17, 2019, to move, which was three weeks away. He said it wasn't him but the board. They were receiving some photography equipment, and the only place they had to store it was the storage room we were living in.

I was confused because I knew who the board was, and they never said anything to my family or me. I looked at him and thanked him for all he's have done. It's okay. God always opens another door when one closes.

When Marvin returned, Pastor Sam told him what he told me. He and his wife prayed for us then we left and went to Grace's house. Once we made it to Grace's house, I was okay because the atmosphere where I was had changed. We ate, laughed, and enjoyed making smores around the bonfire. It was so peaceful, and I enjoyed every moment of it.

I told Grace Pastor Sam said we had three weeks to move. Honestly, I knew that day would come, but I also knew things were different at the church. The atmosphere had changed, and you could feel it. The church was going through some personal issues on its own.

Maybe my family accomplished our assignment, and it was time to move on. Who knows? Our faith was in the Most High, and we trusted Him to guide us.

Katrina Marie
@katrinamarie

I will bless the Lord at all times: His praise
shall continually be in my mouth.

#SteppingOutOnFaith
#CanGodConsiderYou

Psalm 34:1
(King James Version)

Chapter 6

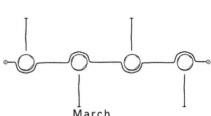

March

Back to the Hotel

t's March 17, 2019, and we had to move out of the church. We packed all our stuff and put most of it back in the storage unit, then back to the Extended Stay hotel we went!

No matter what, I wanted my kids to have as much stability as possible, and that meant staying in the same school in this instance. So with that in mind, I finally decided to tell my son's best friend's mom, Ms. Stacey, about what was happening with us. She graciously offered for Trell to stay with them until we could find a place of our own, and we agreed!

That was a tough decision for me as a mom, but I knew he was in good hands; he was sleeping there just about every weekend anyway. So while Trell stayed with his best friend, Ely, the rest of us stayed at the Extended Stay hotel… with only one car… which meant that I had to make yet again another adjustment to my daily schedule.

Ashley helped us find a bus that would take my daughter to and from school; so thanks to her, we saved time and fuel. Still woke up at 3:00 a.m., took my husband to work, got my daughter ready for school, attended my morning prayer call, went to work, got off work and picked up my husband from work, greeted my daughter after school and we carried on like this for four months. Every day was accounted for.

†††

Then, one day during my prayer time, God told me to record a video about what my family was going through and post it on Facebook.

If I posted it on Facebook, everybody would know about our business, and we were private people concerning our household.

Well, I compromised with God… I did the video, but I posted it in a 'private' Facebook group—my sister's Write to Heal group. The video was titled, *Can God Consider You?*

I will remind you, this happened in 2019, two years prior to the release of this book.*

The message was powerful. I felt good about doing it, but Holy Spirit wouldn't let me rest.

Holy Spirit told me to make it public. I knew the group only had a small number of people in it, so I didn't worry about everyone seeing it; but Holy Spirit convicted me immediately.

> *"We must do what God says even when it might put people in our business or we feel shame."*
> *-@KatrinaMarie*

So, I was obedient and posted the video on my public Facebook page as instructed. There were a lot of responses to that video! My friend, Jackie, even contacted me and told me we could move in with them. They had a 4-bedroom house in Georgia, and we could all have our own room.

✝✝✝

Jackie and her husband were truck drivers and they were always on the road. They opened their home to us and said all we had to do was to accept. The offer sounded good, but we couldn't accept because we didn't want to pull the kids out of school and move to a different state. Marvin was our primary source of income, and he couldn't quit his job. I thanked her but respectfully declined. It wasn't time for us to move.

She told us that the offer was still on the table if we changed our minds. She prayed with me and then invited us for a visit. Now that we agreed!

Jackie had a beautiful home in Dallas, Georgia. The houses in Georgia were huge and not too expensive compared to where we lived. That weekend in Georgia allowed us to pause. We didn't worry about what we were going through. Just enjoyed hanging out with friends. We laughed, talked, and prayed. That weekend made us reconsider moving, but we didn't know how we would do it.

✝✝✝

After the visit with my friend in Georgia, it was time to return to our reality. Every day my routine was the same. I was on a merry-go-round and just wanted to get OFF. I was getting so tired, and some days I cried because I didn't want to go to work.

My sister Jamie and I stayed in contact with each other, and when I felt I was down, I would call her, and she would uplift me and vice versa. We both were going through similar things, so we knew there was a connection. The Most High chose us to go through for a reason, and we would see this thing to the end. Together as sisters. We really leaned on each other.

Faith in The Most High was the only thing keeping us. We both scheduled times that we would pray together and come against some generational curses, bind some things, and loose some things.

We confessed our sins and repented. We knew there was power in prayer and agreement and that we would come out victorious. My flesh wanted to quit, but my faith in God gave me the power to keep moving forward. That's why our eyes should focus on Him, not the circumstance.

✝✝✝

My spirit was lifted, but I struggled with going to work. I always had a good work ethic, so what was happening? When I first got the job, I was so excited, and I just knew we would get the eviction paid off quickly, and we would get a house. Well, that wasn't the case. Living in the hotel was expensive, and my entire check paid for our hotel room, with no money left over. We were paying around $2,000 a month! That was a lot.

I was in prayer one morning and heard the Lord tell me to quit my job. *What? Are you serious?* I couldn't believe what I had heard! *He blessed me with the job, so why would He tell me to quit?*

It didn't make sense, and how are we supposed to pay off the eviction and get a house if I quit my job? So, I ignored what I heard and kept going to work.

The more I went to work, the stronger the feeling of quitting. *Like leave me alone and go away.* I was so torn. I felt as if I was going crazy.

I remember taking off one day and going back to the hotel. I just laid out on the hotel floor in our room and cried. I'm talking about an ugly cry! I laid there looking up at the ceiling.

At that moment, I surrendered everything I felt and gave it to God, saying, "I trust you, Lord. I don't understand, but I trust you."

Can you truly obey God, even if what you hear sounds or makes you look crazy? This faith journey was tough, but I was determined to see it to the end.

†††

One day my friend Brooke reached out to me and told me they were buying a house and wanted to know if we

wanted to take over their payments at their apartment. She said the rent was $1200, and they would move out within a month. I told her I would discuss it with Marvin and get back to her.

We were in July 2019, and I'm just going through the motions. I mean, I had no issues with my job. I was doing an excellent job, and my numbers were all good. Things seemed to be going okay, and then boom. It was time to pay rent again at the hotel, and neither of us had received our paychecks. They were going to make us leave.

The Extended Stay hotel didn't have a setup where you could pay monthly; we had to pay weekly. Thus there were times we had a gap between pay periods. We just prayed about it like we always do, and then Marvin went to talk to the manager about it. Chris told him that we didn't have to pay for the next week. That our next week was free because we always paid on time. *Hallelujah! Thank you, Lord, for answering our prayers.*

We had another week to figure out what to do after that free week's stay. Then I got a text message from my friend, Brooke, about staying in their apartment. She said they closed on their home and had already moved in, and they didn't want to pay both mortgage and rent. Their lease was going to be up at the end of August 2019.

So, I looked at that as a sign from God and told her YES. Plus, the $1200 we needed to pay was cheaper than the $2000 we were paying at the Extended Stay hotel. I explained the payday situation to her and we agreed that my family could move in to the apartment as soon as our stay at the hotel ended.

So, after our last week in the hotel, I met with Brooke and got the keys to the apartment. When I got paid, my check was exactly $1200. The exact amount we needed to give Brooke for the rent. (It was my work bonus plus my hourly wages.)

God had to be a part of that plan!

To show you how amazing God is… When Chad and Brooke arrived to collect the rent money from us, they asked if we would have any money left and if we had food. I told them no but that it would be okay. Chad asked what we were sleeping on, and I told him the floor, but we had covered it. They told me to hold on a minute; they would be back to help us.

When they came back, Chad had a mattress for Shiya and a queen-sized air mattress for Marvin and me. They also gave us two gift cards valued at $100 each to buy food. I am grateful to God for sending these angels to bless our family!

Now because we were no longer in the hotel and living in a different part of town, I was responsible again for taking my daughter, Shiya, to school. Another dilemma, which seemed to come with every move, but I knew we would figure this thing out, too.

School started at 8:45 a.m., and my new work schedule was 7:15 a.m. Now, that was going to be a problem. I knew then that I had to quit my job. *Maybe that's why God told me to quit in the first place because He knew we would be leaving the hotel and there would be a conflict between the school and my job.*

So, I wrote out my resignation notice and took it to my job. I was still uncertain about quitting, but I trusted God. When I got to work, I went straight to my manager's office to give her my notice, but she wasn't in. I waited for my supervisor to give it to him, but he wasn't in either.

I'm like, Lord, if I don't give them this notice today, I might not bring it back tomorrow!

My supervisor finally came in around 11:00 a.m. I gave him my two-week notice, and he was shocked. He said, "But you are doing such an amazing job." He asked if it was the job, and I told him no, it was personal. Then he asked if it would help to work from home, and I told him no.

Then he asked to meet with me privately, and I told him what my family was going through. I also told him that I wasn't passionate about the job either and that I thought if I had a job, it would speed up the process for my family to get our own place. I told him when you are doing what you are passionate about, it is never 'work.'

He then told me working there wasn't his passion either. He loved comic books and wanted to open his own comic bookstore one day, but that job paid the bills. He said he would pray for my family, and if I ever needed a reference for a job, just reach out.

My two weeks remaining on the job were shortened because I had vacation time on the books that needed to be used, so I worked only five days out of two weeks. My last day was August 08, 2019.

My team hosted a party in my honor and wished me well. One sad part about leaving was the relationship I built with my team, but I can't tell you how relieved I was and how much peace I got when I left. That peace let me know I did the right thing.

"See, I believe God allowed me to get that job to show me I wasn't in control... He was." -@KatrinaMarie

I worked that job for eight months, and it didn't get us any closer to getting a home or paying off the eviction. All of my money went into staying in that Extended Stay hotel. I didn't have the power to fix my situation, but God did. He was putting me in a position to solely trust Him.

The wilderness is where He humbles us and checks the motives of our hearts. I'm so glad for this journey because it has changed me and my relationship with The Most High.

†††

We knew we would be at the apartment for 30 days, so that was a relief. I used that time to saturate in the Word of God, and on occasion, I would go to the training center where Chad and Brooke taught.

I spent those 30 days praying, fasting, and listening for instructions. Now Chad and Brooke offered to renew their lease so we could stay there, but it would cost more. I knew we couldn't afford the rent because I was no longer working, so we turned down the offer.

I knew some people thought I was crazy because I quit my job and we were homeless. They couldn't believe God told me to quit when He knew our situation. I knew what I heard, and I had to be obedient to and listen to HIM, not people.

"For I know the plans I have for you," declares the Lord, "plans to prosper you and not to harm you, plans to give you hope and a future." (Jeremiah 29:11, New International Version)

It didn't say *people* knew the plans. After our 30 days at the apartment, we returned to the hotel. That's right, we went back to where we started. The only difference was that we stayed at an actual hotel, not an Extended Stay.

I was sad because Shiya had no stable place to be, but Trell did. By the time she settled, we were moving again, so she went to stay at one of her friends' house. I still took her to school and picked her up, but at least she was in a stable environment.

Living in an actual hotel wasn't that bad. We had access to a free breakfast every morning. It had a swimming pool, jacuzzi, gym and a place we could wash our clothes. To me, God just upgraded us because we didn't have any of these amenities at the Extended Stay.

Overall, I can say we were Blessed! We still stayed in contact with some of our friends we met living at the church. After about two weeks of staying at the hotel, Chef K contacted us, and she offered us to stay at her house for the weekend to give us a break from paying the cost of living in a hotel. So, once we checked out, we went to her house. This was September 2019.

I was so grateful to her for opening her home to us, and I was excited that God provided her with her own place as well because she was homeless at one point too. We met Chef K at the church and became friends. I also got a chance to work with her in the kitchen; may I say, she is an excellent cook. She is a strong woman of God and has the heart to help those in need.

What was supposed to be a weekend pause ended up being over a month. While at Chef K, I reached out to my sister, Jamie, and told her where we were. She invited us to visit her in Atlanta (she had just recently moved there herself), so we took her up on the invite!

Due to previous engagements, the kids couldn't go, so Marvin and I took the trip to Georgia. We made arrangements with Chef K, left Gallatin, Tennessee, and headed to Atlanta, Georgia. Once we got there, my sister and I hugged each other tightly because we hadn't seen each other in a long time. I was so excited to see her.

She even had dinner waiting on us. She made us her famous spaghetti, and it was so good. That was a Friday night. The next day she took us to the mall, and we had lunch at The Cheesecake Factory. The food was delicious!

There was so much peace at my sister's house. It felt as if it was where I was supposed to be. We stayed up watching movies, laughing, talking, and enjoying being in each other's presence. Even my husband Marvin stated he could feel the peace. We slept so well while we were there. We got some much-needed rest.

It's now Sunday, and we must head back to Tennessee. I didn't want to go. I hugged my sister Jamie so tight before leaving. I didn't want to leave the space we were just in. I cried tremendously. The pain I felt in my chest was unbearable. She prayed for us and told me it was going to be okay. "Just Breathe!" She said.

I took a couple of deep breaths, and she told my husband, Marvin, "Take care of my sister." He said, "I will."

We texted Chef K and let her know we were headed back. Once we returned to Gallatin, Tennessee, my sister reached out to me. She wanted us to come and live with her in Atlanta. She stated the pain she felt from me when we left almost took her out. She was opening her home up to us. I looked at that again as a sign from God because this was the second time the door was opened for us to move to Georgia. That time I wasn't going to miss out!

There were some things we had to get in place before moving to Atlanta, but I gave my sister a YES! You never know God's plans for you, so we must trust the process.

✝✝✝

To get through anything in life, you must have faith. God allowed us to meet some amazing people along this journey. Each person He allowed us to meet impacted our lives in an infectious way. To not only talk about the love of Christ, but show it with actions was just a breath of fresh air.

It had been over 2 years since we were evicted, and we were still on this faith journey. I can tell you we wouldn't have made it this far without faith, the angels' assistance, and those divine connections The Most High set up on the way.

The Lord uses every part of our life for His glory. Nothing is wasted. All things are working for your good. Even the things you don't understand. The Most High always finishes what He starts!

Katrina Marie
@katrinamarie

The Lord is close to the brokenhearted and saves those who are crushed in spirit.

#SteppingOutOnFaith
#CanGodConsiderYou

Psalm 34:18
(New International Version)

Chapter 7

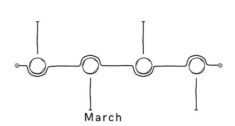

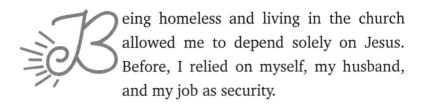

Realizing Our True Dependance

eing homeless and living in the church allowed me to depend solely on Jesus. Before, I relied on myself, my husband, and my job as security.

We get so comfortable with our lives that we have tricked ourselves into believing we are in control of our own security. We start solely relying on ourselves and never really acknowledge Jesus in our lives.

We get so comfortable that we don't even give Jesus first place in our lives. We think we are doing well because we go to church every Sunday, bible class, tithe, and do good deeds, but what is your motive for doing those things?

Is it so you can check it off your to-do list to say you did it, or do you really want a heart like our Father in Heaven? Do you really want to have an intimate relationship with Him? Can you really set aside your self-centeredness and surrender your life to Jesus?

We have allowed the enemy to trick us into thinking that if we just work harder, go back to school, work three jobs, buy a house, and live off of the world's resources, we can live a good life. See, that's a lie.

I'm not saying Jesus doesn't want us to have all these things, but He doesn't want material things to be our focus. He wants to have a relationship with us. He wants to be a part of our lives. When we accept Him in our lives, we no longer live from the world's resources but from the resources of where we are from. We are from the kingdom of Heaven.

John 15:19 says, "If ye were of the world, the world would love his own: but because ye are not of the world, but I

have chosen you out of the world, therefore the world hateth you."

There are benefits for those who accept Jesus as your Lord and Savior. First, we are entitled to an inheritance. Just imagine our Heavenly Father has an unlimited supply of anything and everything you need. Because you are now in covenant with The Most High, you inherit these benefits.

I don't know about you, but that is some excellent news. See, that's why the enemy doesn't want you to know who you indeed are because it will keep you from accessing all the promises, plans, and your purpose from God. You will realize your power because of Jesus, who lives in you.

This journey has taught me that God has always been speaking to me, but I never took the time to stop and listen.

I struggled to ask God to speak to me daily because I needed to hear from Him. I focused so much on hearing Him audibly that I forgot the bible was Him speaking to me too.

As I started saturating in the Word of God, I realized the bible is alive. God was speaking to me, and I never took the time to open the bible to hear what He had to say. God was speaking loud and clear.

God has a Word for you concerning any issue you are having. *All I can say is Wow!* I am enjoying my relationship with my new best friend, Jesus. Every day I get to spend time getting to know Him because He already knows everything about me.

> *"I have gained so much wisdom while on this journey. The wilderness is not so bad after all."*
> *-@KatrinaMarie*

†††

We have been taught the wilderness is a bad place, but the wilderness is a place where God humbles you and truly sees where your heart is. He wants to know if you genuinely have faith in Him or if He can trust you. We can say we have all of the faith in the world, and give God the glory and bless His name when things are going well, but can you still give Him praise, glory and honor when things are not going well? When your back is against the wall?

We pray and ask God for things and God wants to give them to us, but if our hearts are not right, He knows we would cause more damage to our lives. And because He loves us so much, He doesn't want to see us hurt.

Sometimes He gives us what we ask for just so we can see that we didn't need it in the first place. If He gave us everything we asked for without testing us, then we wouldn't appreciate it and forget it was God that made it happen and not ourselves; but if He allowed for us to go through the wilderness and suffer a little, then once He brings us out and blesses us for our faithfulness, then we would remember that God was the One who delivered us. Our praise, honor and glory then goes to its rightful owner, God.

We have tricked ourselves into believing we are in control of our lives, but we are not. God is in complete control, and we can only do what He allows us to do.

We are nothing without Him, but we are everything with Him.

✝✝✝

I'm falling in love with my Father in Heaven all over again and I'm so happy about it. I find myself thinking about Him more and more. Oh, how I wish I had this kind of relationship with Him years earlier, but there is no time like the present. He is our Present Help (Psalm 46:1). He has truly captured my heart and now I want more of Him. He is my everything.

Psalm 46:1 says, "God is our refuge and strength, an ever-present help in trouble."

We have gotten so used to living in the physical realm that we forget about the spiritual realm. We treat Jesus like a trend. When something first comes out, we are all excited about it; it's hot, we tell everyone to check it out, and we will spend our last to get it. But once we get used to it and someone mentions it, the thrill is gone. We move on to the next thing that's trending.

If our Heavenly Father is giving us what we want, like healing, performing miracles, blessings, and being our personal genie, we want to claim Him and rock with Him. The minute we go through something or feel our prayers aren't being answered, we want to say there is no God and put Him on the back burner.

Do you really love God, or are we rolling with Him just to get what we can from Him? Can you say you love

Him just for Him and not for material things? Check your Motives! Ask God to examine your heart.

This harsh truth slapped me in the face. I had to do a self-inventory of myself to see where the core of my heart lies. I had to repent and ask for forgiveness for a lot of things that I did but didn't realize because I was living and relying on the resources from the physical realm.

Still, when you ask God to show you, you better be ready for what you are about to see... it will put you on your face with a heart of repentance.

✝✝✝

I was raised in the church all my life and thought I knew it all, but this journey gave me a new awakening and let me know I didn't know anything. Yes, I'm saved, love Jesus, know scriptures, and am filled with Holy Spirit, but my personal relationship with Him was questionable.

I'm so glad I have come to myself, and God is leading me in the right direction. I'm getting stronger, and so are my husband and children. Our lives have been impacted by this journey and those we have met while on this journey. This journey wasn't just about us, but those God has allowed to be a part of our family.

Sometimes you just gotta laugh at the devil and say, "You tried it!" -Katrina Marie

We have built new relationships, and God has given us the ability to meet the needs of others by using the skills and gifts He has given us. To hear people talk about the love of Jesus and show the love of Jesus by their actions is a beautiful thing.

We are the hands and feet of Jesus, and we are to walk the way He walked. We are representatives and ambassadors of Christ, so we must represent Him well. We are children of The Most High, royalty, and we shouldn't do anything that will tarnish the family's name.

✝✝✝

I believe God said, "Have you considered the Brown family? They are a family of faith; no matter what they go through, they will continue to believe in Me. They might cry, get discouraged, or even question their sanity sometimes, but they will continue to stand on My Word, which is their foundation.

They may sway to the left, right, front and back like the trees, but their foundation will not crumble because their faith is in Me. Family and friends may not understand some of their decisions, but they will still choose to obey Me. Their faith is in Me, and not man."

I can picture once this is all over, God saying, "Well done, my faithful servants."

✝✝✝

We go through things in life and ask God, why me? God is saying, why NOT you? He knows you because He is Omniscient (all-knowing). He knows you can make it through. I am honored to be considered by The Most High because He knows He has already equipped me for a time like this.

All of the small tests were preparing us for the big test. He was training and getting us in shape because He knew the test could make or break us. *We lived in a church, hotels, and random places, but I believe God has a home with The Brown Family's name on it!*

✝✝✝

Living at the church allowed us to build relationships with some incredible people. Yes, some were addicts and homeless but guess what we didn't care. Knowing their stories gave me a heart of compassion for them, and I wanted to see them healed. God allowed me to share healing and freedom with them. That's what they needed. They wanted it but didn't know how to get it.

If someone told you that they had the cure for you and you would be healed and could walk in it and all you had to do was surrender your life to Christ, repent and accept Him as your Lord and Savior, would you want it? But of course, you would. There is nothing our Father wouldn't do for us because He loves us.

Just to think He would leave the 99 just to come and find me is mind-blowing. When I hurt, He hurts, and He wants nothing more than to rescue us; but we have to say 'Yes.' He will, in no way, force Himself on us. He wants us to freely give ourselves to Him and have a relationship with Him.

What if the reason God allowed for this to happen to us so who could minister to His people or stretch us because He knows we can do so much more? We needed to get out of our comfort zone because we couldn't grow that way. We had to get uncomfortable, and being misplaced was uncomfortable, but we found joy in the journey.

This put us in a position to solely have faith in God. God had us in a position where our lives were dependent upon Him. We couldn't do anything without Him. He was our everything. Without Him, we were inadequate.

God intends that our trials will drive those who believe in Him to greater dependency on Him by showing us our own inadequacy. God has everything that we need if we are willing to seek Him for it.

This journey has also taught us that we are nothing apart from Jesus. When we learn to embrace our helplessness and allow Jesus to merge with us, we solely depend on Him. Because we allow Jesus to live in us, we now have our Father's nature—which means we have everything we need.

Having His nature causes us to do what He would do—think like Him, talk like Him, see like Him and shine light in the lives of those who are in darkness. We go through trials sometimes because God is increasing and strengthening our faith. We shouldn't always look at things negatively but embrace them and ask God *what am I to learn from this experience?*

Believe me, God can be traced in every situation. Through trials, we as believers learn to withstand the pressure until God removes it at His appointed time. Faith isn't falling apart when trials come. I stand in faith knowing my identity is found in The Most High and His Word is always true. Joy comes from God, not your circumstances or material things. I am so grateful that we are surrounded by the arms of the Father. I am a daughter of the King, and I am glad about it. He is my #1 Passion!

Katrina Marie
@katrinamarie

Who is this King of glory? The Lord strong and mighty, the Lord mighty in battle.

#SteppingOutOnFaith
#CanGodConsiderYou

Psalm 24:8
(New International Version)

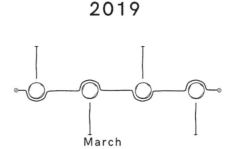

Chapter 8

March

Reflections

No one must tell me God is a provider, way maker, and promise keeper because I know for myself. There is no limit to what God can do.

What He has done for The Brown Family, He will do it for you. The question is, what do you believe God for? What are your dreams? Are you willing to go all the way with Him no matter what?

Everything we want in life is possible, but it takes faith and works to make those possibilities happen.

Hebrews 11:1 says, "Now faith is confidence in what we hope for and assurance about what we do not see."

Why did I write this book?

I knew there was someone out there that needed this. They need to know God is a living God and that He can demonstrate His power in their life.

They need to know miracles, favor, angels, grace, and mercy is for everyone that believes and has faith.

They need to know their identity is found in Him.

I wanted to tell them don't quit and keep the faith even when their situation doesn't look good. Faith moves God, and there is no limit to what you can achieve through Christ.

Believe in yourself and know God uses everything in our life for His glory. Nothing is wasted. Look at it as training to get you to your next or your purpose. It's never too late to start back dreaming. To achieve something, you must first visualize it and then write it down.

How can you get anywhere when you don't know where you are going? The key is to keep moving and trust The Most High will lead and guide you where you need to be. I mean, He is the Good Shepherd.

See, I was fed up with the life I was living. I knew there was more to me than what I was doing. No one wants to just exist or survive. I wanted to LIVE and THRIVE. I wanted to help those who were hurting, depressed, and feeling like giving up.

People need to know they are not alone. If we told our stories more, maybe it wouldn't be so many people lost.

I mean, no one just woke and arrived. All storms are not bad. Some storms increase your faith, bring you closer to God, rely on God alone, and see God demonstrate His extraordinary powers in your life.

Even though storms cause destruction, sometimes God is there in the storm with you. We are never alone. His presence is always with us. Just keep the faith no matter what you are experiencing in the natural. Keep your eyes focused on Him and stand on His Word, your true foundation. It will never give in.

God is our Father, and He always takes care of His children. Trust that He knows what's best for us because

He is our Creator. There is nothing God would withhold from us because He loves us.

Our minds will never understand the unconditional love God has for us. One way you know He loves us is because John 3:16 tells us, *"For God so loved the world that He gave his one and only Son, that whoever believes in Him shall not perish but have eternal life."*

I had a big dream for myself and my family. That's why I had to change my mindset. I knew I wanted to touch lives, have generational wealth, a house, and be able to sow seeds into others. I mean, I want my pockets to be able to bless people. So I am a kingdom ambassador. I have worked for over 20 years.

In the same way, I worked hard and invested in the companies I worked for; I could go hard and invest in myself and do what I love to do. I have a servant's heart, so I love serving others. I was tired of doing the same old things and not getting anywhere.

See, I didn't receive anything from my job because I was always on time, worked hard, worked overtime, and went over and beyond the call of duty. I worked every holiday and weekend and had no time for God or my family. I missed out on a lot. I knew my life would change, but only if I stopped living in fear and stepped out on faith. The only way to get different results is to do something different.

REMINDER

See, you can have anything you want in life if you are willing to give up the thought that you can't have it.

@katrinamarie   #TheEncourager

God believes in you, but you must believe in yourself. I'm not saying that it will be easy if you decide to step out on faith. What I'm saying is if you fall, God will be there to pick you up and dust you off.

I don't know precisely where God directs me, but I trust the process. My future is bright, and God is positioning me for greatness. I don't take credit for where I am. God gets all the glory and praise. God is the one responsible for my victory. God is the one who gave my family and me the tools we needed to ride out the storm, and I am so grateful.

Words cannot express the joy and peace I am feeling inside. I want to live a life pleasing unto God and infectious to those I encounter. Choosing this lifestyle meant I had to be set apart from people because I didn't need negativity in my life or anyone diminishing my dreams.

✝✝✝

Until now, my immediate family and in-laws didn't know what we were going through. **Sometimes you must move in silence.**

We didn't want them telling us we shouldn't have moved or I shouldn't have quit my jobs. They probably would have wanted us to move back to Mississippi. We had to silence the noise from our surroundings and tune in to The Most High's voice. That was the only way we were going to hear clearly.

It's not good to tell everyone what God is doing in your life because they will try to get you to change your mind or tell you what you should do. The Lord tells us to seek Him first and that He knows the plans He has for us.

My family didn't look like what we were going through! We still smiled, had joy, and may I say we were dressed blessed. No one ever would have figured we were in a storm.

When you are claiming victory, you can't look defeated. Remember, our faith was in God, so we lived like we were victorious already.

†††

When in a storm, you don't have to look like what you are going through. You must remain confident that you will see the glory of the Lord working miracles in your life.

The storm is behind us, but because we went through the storm, our faith is stronger, we saw God perform miracles, and we have a closer relationship with Him. We saw Him make ways out of no ways, and we learned that He is our true provider. I wouldn't change that for the world!

I have a new outlook on life. God gives me spiritual wisdom and knowledge daily so I may have an intimate relationship with Him and walk in my gift with confidence, passion, purpose, and effectiveness.

It's not me doing the work but God working through me to deliver the message to you. My question to you is, are you ready to experience God on a whole new level?

I'm not talking about religion but 'relationship.'

Do you want the promises of God to show up in your life? Do you want to use the gifts God planted in you? Do you want to become a better you? Do you want to know your identity?

Guess what? You have the power to do it! All it takes is for you to surrender, believe you can, and then take the leap of faith. '*I can't*' and '*fear*' shouldn't be in your vocabulary because 2 Timothy 1:7 (KJV) says, "*For God hath not given us the spirit of fear; but of power, and of love, and of a sound mind.*" So, we have no excuse as to why we can't do something.

You must ask yourself, how bad do you want to see a change in your life? Now, suppose you are comfortable where you are in life. In that case, this isn't for you, but if you are tired of being on a merry-go-round, feeling incomplete, lost, broke, disgusted, tired, existing, just surviving, depressed, unvalued, and you have this strong feeling inside that this can't be the life God wants me to live, then my story is for you.

Some friends, family members, co-workers, or people will tell you you are crazy, but don't listen to them. Your life and future are at stake, and you have no time for negativity. Just pray for them and keep moving.

Remember, sometimes we must move in silence. Some people just don't believe, and that's okay. Some people need to see proof, and some don't. I'm proof of what the mercy of God can do. He took the old me and made me new. I don't get upset because people don't believe anymore. I simply say that their mindsets need to be renewed or reprogrammed. They haven't had an encounter with God because every encounter with God makes us better.

> *"You can NOT have an encounter with God and remain the same." -@KatrinaMarie*

I had stinking thinking too, and I was raised in the church. Renewing and reprogramming your mind is a process. The mind has thought the wrong way for so long that it feels right when it's not. So we must ask God daily to renew our minds.

Romans 12:2 says, "Do not conform to the pattern of this world, but be transformed by the renewing of your mind. Then you will be able to test and approve what God's will is—his good, pleasing and perfect will."

Our minds can be renewed, but we really must want it. Again, how bad do you want it? Change is a journey. It takes time, work, energy, sacrifices, faith, strength, deliverance, repentance, forgiveness, trust, honesty, and patience. Even though it seems like a lot, the reward is worth it.

And let us not grow weary while doing good, for in due season we shall reap if we do not lose heart. (Galatian 6:9)

That's why we must keep pressing. Someone is waiting on you because you are the answer to their prayers. They need access to the gift God put in you. My journey wasn't easy, but my faith in God allowed me to get through it.

Now look at me.

I'm more confident, and my identity was found in The Most High. I know who I am now.

I wasn't an honor student; I was molested at a young age, ran away from home, abused, had suicidal thoughts, was a teen mom, and had no future. Look at me now!

I am a daughter of a King, married, beautiful kids, a co-author of a book, an author of my own book, and a servant of The Most High. I get to touch so many lives and encourage those that I meet. None of this would be possible if I never decided to step out on faith and trust God's process for my family on our new journey.

We didn't know what we were stepping into, but we knew we wanted something better. We knew we had God, His word, our faith, and each other. That's all we needed, and that's all you need.

†††

So now that you have the key, what will you do with it? Now that you know you have the power to speak and change your life, what things are you going to speak? Life or Death? Negative or Positive? Fear or Faith? God or Yourself? At some point, you will have to make a choice. I pray you to make it today while you still have breath in your lungs.

I don't want you looking back and saying, *I should have done this or did that.* **The time is now.**

It was God who put it on my heart to share my testimony with you about how awesome He is and how powerful He can be. If God can do it for me, He can do it for you. All God is waiting on is for you to say YES!

I know you feel it because a voice is talking to you even as you read this book. That voice is the Holy Spirit which is the voice of God. You have watched people around you get healed, delivered, transformed, blessed, and live life to the fullest. **It's your time.** *Why not you?* God loves you too!

So, will you surrender today? He is waiting on you. He loves you and wants the best for you, but He won't force you because He has given you free will to choose. Plus, He is such a gentleman, ladies. He wants you to freely give yourself to Him. No strings attached.

✝✝✝

God has a plan and purpose for your life. Just go ahead and surrender and enjoy the peace He gives. He wants to free you in your mind and heart. It's never too late with God. He is always standing there with open arms, waiting patiently on you.

There are so many possibilities out there for you. All you got to do is step out on faith. If I had never stepped out on faith, I would have missed out on all the blessings and opportunities God had for me. My eyes have been opened to another realm of God, and I have experienced a new love for God I have never had before. I love God so much! None can compare to Him.

God is a great God, a mighty defender, faithful, merciful, provider, friend, comforter, awesome, truth, healer, mind regulator, way maker, miracle worker, promise keeper, peace, strength, all-powerful, graceful, hope, shepherd, teacher, shelter and I can go on and on, but these are just a few that I witnessed on my journey.

Once you get in the presence of God and get a glimpse of what is in store, you will be drawn entirely to God. You will experience a feeling you have never felt before. That's what the power of The Most High can do in your life. No one can make you feel like that. Man can't compare to God!

†††

Truth is, I didn't have to share my story with you, but because I was being obedient to God, I had to. God gets all the glory for this book because He was the one orchestrating the whole journey. Believe me when I say there were a lot of tears, hurt, frustration, and weakness in the journey. But, we purposed in our hearts to keep the faith and never quit. We loved God too much to quit.

What if Jesus quit on us by not going to the cross because the pain He endured was too much? That would mean our sins wouldn't have been forgiven, and we wouldn't have access to God. We would have no right to salvation. Because He loved us so much, He became the lamb of sacrifice so we would have salvation and be redeemed.

When we deserved death, He took our place. Now, that's love! So, God didn't quit or give up on us, so we couldn't give up on Him. When things got tough, we kept our eyes on Him and our future, not on our current situations. We kept declaring that *we trust You, Lord, have faith, and believe Your Word is true.* We have done so much in life to please ourselves and others, but the more we got to know God, the more we wanted to please Him.

✝✝✝

My job is not to force you to believe. My job is to simply give my testimony about what God did for my family and me. Nobody but God could do the amazing miracles that took place in our lives. It's even hard for me to try and explain it to you. How can you explain miracles and supernatural breakthroughs? I have one name for you, which is The Most High.

Now He has many names, but I now call Him "Yah" because I have an intimate relationship with Him.

I also call Him "Father". There is no way to give my testimony without talking about God. He is the One who is in control of all things. We can't do anything without God. That's why I am so excited to share my testimony and journey with you.

Once again, if you want to grow and experience life like never, it's time for you to take that leap of faith. Start back dreaming again. Now the road may get a little rough, but God had already gone before you and made every crooked place straight, every rough path smooth and brought every high place low. He has everything all mapped out. All you got to do is step.

When you get tired, crawl if you must; just don't stop moving and don't quit. Keep your eyes on God, and you won't sink. See, a storm came into my life, and fear tried to paralyze me, but Jesus gave me peace amidst the storm.

The storm beat against us from all sides, causing pain and discouragement sometimes, but it couldn't destroy us because we were standing on the Word of God.

Sometimes I felt like I was drowning, but it was then that Jesus reached out His hands and pulled me to safety. When I felt like I was all alone and didn't think I could go any further, it was then that Jesus breathed life back into me. I can walk through fire and not get burned because the fire isn't designed to burn me but refine me—so when I come out, I will be pure as gold, and so will you. Storms come to make us stronger, not hurt us.

✝✝✝

I love that God loves us so much that we can call on Him anytime. He never sleeps. He is available to talk to us 24 hours a day and 365 days a year.

God is always working in our lives, even when we can't see or feel Him. He never stops working. He never clocks out or takes a break. He never gets tired, and He will never ever give up on us.

It doesn't matter what we have or have not done. We can always repent, and He is faithful enough to forgive our sins, make us white as snow, and throw our sins in the sea of forgetfulness. That's love!

How many people do you know that will do that for you? Let me answer that for you, NONE!

If you only let God into your heart and let Him take residence there, you will be changed. To say that I not only know God but have a relationship with Him is the best feeling ever. I am the joy of my Father's heart, and that's a great feeling.

Guess what? You are the joy of His heart also. I now have a sense of peace that I have never had, and I know it came from accepting Jesus and Holy Spirit into my heart. Once you feel the presence of God moving in your life, you don't want that feeling to go away. Repenting, forgiveness, healing, and deliverance can offer you freedom.

When I cried out to God, He heard my cry, and a weight was lifted from me. My heart was no longer heavy. Wow! That is what freedom feels like. I feel light as a feather.

I'm not complete yet, but I thank God I'm not where I used to be. I am a new creature in Him. God is still shaping and sharpening me into someone great. I'm not ashamed of who I am anymore.

God allowed me to go through that broken stage so that He could put me back together and be the woman of God I am today. Faith is the key; without it, we can't make it. I have joy in my heart now, and it feels so good. I love this joy because Jesus gave it to me so no one can take it away. Even though I didn't know my earthly father, my spiritual Father in Heaven has always provided for me. He saved me, and there aren't enough words I can say to let Him know how grateful I am to have Him in my life. I wouldn't be here without Him. I can't imagine living my life apart from Him. God loves me, and He loves you too!

So, last, I have one question left for you, **Can God Consider You?**

To be continued…

Katrina Marie, Author

CashApp: $Encourager79

About the Author

ife, mother, daughter, sister, and friend is not even the tip of the iceberg to describe Katrina Marie! Affectionately known as *The Encourager*, Katrina Marie has spent a great deal of her spiritual journey interceding for others. She's a master prayer interceder!

Twenty years in the food industry, a lifetime of servitude, Katrina Marie has overcome rape, abuse, neglect, homelessness, miscarriages, depression, suicidal ideation, panic attacks, financial hardship, death and grief, abandonment by biological father... and yet, she still has a heart to love and serve God's people! She's the epitome of faith, but make no mistake, she's fully aware from whence her help comes from!

You haven't heard the last of Katrina Marie. Her faith journey continues.

Acknowledgements

I wish to extend my special thanks to Black Seed LLC for publishing my book. You helped me from the beginning to the end and ensured I finished the book. You all are so dope!

I would also like to acknowledge my sister, Jamie, who is the owner of Black Seeds LLC. Without you and your Company, my book would have never come to fruition. Thank you for always loving and supporting me and allowing me to be my true self.

I appreciate the time you have invested in helping to get my story out to the world. Even though I was your sister, you did not treat me differently. I was your client and was treated with the utmost respect.

Thank you for your professionalism and integrity. I love you much!

CPSIA information can be obtained
at www.ICGtesting.com
Printed in the USA
LVHW071243081222
734780LV00047B/2129